XI. Olympische
Spiele Berlin
1936

GW00367386

ATHLETICS
at the
EMPIRE STADIUM WEMBLEY
SATURDAY AUGUST 7TH 1948

OFFICIAL PROGRAMME - ONE SHILLING

XV OLYMPIA HELSINKI 1952

YLEISURHEILU
ATHLETISME · ATHLETICS · FRI-IDROTT

OLYMPIASTADION
HELSINKI · HELSINGFORS

SUNNUNTAI · DIMANCHE
SUNDAY · SÖNDAG   27. 7.

PÄIVÄOHJELMA · PROGRAMME JOURNALIER
DAILY PROGRAMME · DAGSPROGRAM   100 mk

OLYMPIC GAMES
MELBOURNE   AUSTRALIA
1956

ATHLETICS

MAIN STADIUM
(Melbourne Cricket Ground)

SATURDAY, 1ST DECEMBER, 1956

OFFICIAL PROGRAMME - ONE SHILLING

John
My very good friend

THANKS AND NO THANKS
MR HITLER!

a man to be admired !

The Dorothy Odam-Tyler Story

Quadruple Olympian 1936, 1948, 1952 & 1956

Best wishes
Mike

MIKE FLEET

Foreword by Dick Fosbury

Front cover: Dorothy winning one of her titles in South of England Championships in the 1930s. Photo from Getty Image and artwork by Alice Chandler.

Published in August 2015 by emp3books Ltd
Norwood House, Elvetham Road, Fleet, GU51 4HL

This book has been very carefully researched and sources checked as fully as possible.

Acknowledgement is given to all known sources.

ISBN-13: 978-1-910734-04-9

Dorothy Odam-Tyler (1920-2014)
(Gerry Cranham photo)

The Author

Mike Fleet is a former Great Britain athlete and World Student Games and Commonwealth Games 800m finalist, whose 1964 Tokyo Olympic dreams were thwarted by injury. A retired school-master, he is still very active as a long-time senior UKA athletics coach, helping runners, jumpers and throwers and also working as athletics coach at the Trinity and Whitgift Schools in Croydon. He is UKA track and field official, announcer, and club committee man with Croydon Harriers, his only club, which he joined in 1956. In his heyday, he was disappointed not to achieve Olympic selection but now appreciates how much else can be achieved through sport, as evidenced in his self-effacing autobiography.

Mike did gain vicarious satisfaction through the Olympic achievements of his former protégé, Martyn Rooney. He also relished his role as coach-in-residence to some delightful athletes from the Island of Dominica during their stay in England, prior to the London 2012 Olympics. Later, the great honour of being nominated to "run" a leg in the Olympic Torch Relay through West Croydon was the icing on the cake.

A large chocolate bar is still up for grabs by the first athlete to break Mike's Croydon Harriers' 800m record of 1:48.2 set in 1962. He sees this time as being well within the capability of Rooney, the current European 400m Champion, and still hopes Martyn will move up to two laps, where his presence could prove a serious threat to the current world leaders.

His writing of Dorothy's story, which she requested after attending the launch of his first book, "I Also Ran by Mike Who?" as a VIP, led him on an interesting journey both with her, her family and her fellow Olympians.

Mike had to forgive Dorothy for her excited claims to be writing the book herself after she acted as starter for the 2012 London Marathon. She confided to Sue Barker in her post-duty live TV interview, "I am now writing my book!"

Certainly Mike owes Dorothy and her family a great debt of gratitude for allowing him several years of their confidence, and access to literally piles of press cuttings, photographs and memorabilia. He has found it very rewarding and as Dorothy is no longer with us, Mike feels fortunate indeed to have had the opportunity to record her story for posterity.

Photographic advisor Gerry Cranham (left) and the author compare their Olympic torches (1948 and 2012 respectively) (Mark Cranham photo)

Dick Fosbury and Dorothy share a joke

Foreword

by
Dick Fosbury

**Olympic Gold High Jump Gold Medallist,
Mexico City 1968 2.24m (7' 4¼")
Olympic and United States Record**

In 2010, my wife and I took a train from London out to Loughborough University for a high jump clinic I was to give. Dorothy came up for the afternoon to chat with us and share some of her memories, bringing her Olympic silver medals and her 1936 Berlin torch.

Dorothy told story after story, and made a point of telling us how Babe Didrikson was disqualified on one of her jumps in 1932 because her head went over the bar first. Babe had won the Silver medal, but later admitted she had used the same technique the whole time.

I met Dorothy again at a British journalists' luncheon a few years ago while I was in the UK leading up to the 2012 Olympics. She told the press during her interview how my technique was illegal, which got a big chuckle from those present, including me. I recall that every time a coach would see me jump for the first time, they would get out the rule book to see if I was doing something illegal. I was much luckier than Dorothy on that account, because by the 1960's we had consistent rules on technique, of which the most important was that the jumper had to take off on one foot.

In 2004, I was honored by being asked to induct Alice Coachman into the US Olympic Hall of Fame, her daughter accepting the award on her behalf. I finally met Alice in 2012 at the US Olympic Committee's 100-day send-off for the London Games in New York's Times Square, where there was a ceremony honoring American athletes from the 1948 London Games. Alice won the Gold Medal in 1948 and Dorothy the silver; she (*Alice*) was not only the first African American woman to win a gold medal, but also the first black female athlete to win Olympic gold.

I am so pleased that Dorothy's story is being told along with Alice's and some of the other great women athletes of her time, and that Dorothy's own myriad stories will not be lost. She was vivacious, witty, opinionated and charming, and I trust you will enjoy reading Mike's book about her amazing life and achievements.

Dick Fosbury
January 2015

Dick Fosbury and Dorothy watch a high jump demonstration in 2010 (Job King Photo)

Contents

INTRODUCTION

Twenty years an active Olympian
"Heil Who?.. God save the King!"
"I never did do diplomacy"
The Dorothy Odam-Tyler story

"Would you write mine for me?", the silver-haired old lady asked.

The seeds for "Thanks, No Thanks to Mr Hitler" were sown by Dorothy herself, when having, as a VIP, attended the launch of my autobiography, "I Also Ran by Mike Who?", she asked if I would write her story. So began four privileged, productive and fascinating years of interview and research. ....

The title of this book refers to the influence Adolf Hitler had on Dorothy's athletic career. At Hitler's amazingly spectacular but politically charged Nazi Olympic Games in Berlin in 1936, she sprang into the limelight, taking the high jump silver medal. Then at the tender age of sixteen she seemed to be on the brink of many years of success. Unfortunately, the very same Mr Hitler took the world into a war, which brought untold horrors to millions. Although it seems minor by comparison, Dorothy and many other aspiring athletes were never able to fulfil their potential. Surely two Olympic golds might have been on the cards but for the War?

During World War 2, I became well aware of the infamous Hitler's bombing devilry in South London, then a world of air raid sirens, dashes to the shelter and hearing fortunately fairly distant explosions from the impact of V1 Flying Bombs or "Doodlebugs" as they became dubbed. During lulls between raids I excitedly searched for bomb fragments and other shrapnel.

Immediately after the war ended, as luck would have it, I discovered a newspaper which emerged from under the carpet of our family home. There was a page featuring a photo of a strange looking man, identified by my father as Jesse Owens, the 1936 legendary Olympic hero, not falling as I imagined, but doing a "special start" at the beginning of a great race!

This was the first time I had become aware of black people and the first I had learned of a sport called athletics. Three more years passed before I realised that women took part in athletics too. The name Blankers-Koen was on many admiring lips as Fanny, the "Flying Dutchwoman", hit the headlines during the London Olympics of 1948.

Sadly, I remained blissfully unaware of a Mitcham housewife and mother, who had by then won her second Olympic high jump silver medal after a gap of twelve years.

At the time of the 1952 Helsinki Olympics, I read that a bright British hope, Roger Bannister, had been well beaten in the 1500m by an almost unknown Luxembourger, Josy Barthel, and that the seemingly indestructible Czechoslovakian Emil Zatopek had notched up an incredible triple gold tally in the 5000m, 10000m and marathon. The third Olympic appearance of Dorothy, the high jumping housewife and mother, and still a Mitcham resident not surprisingly eluded the notice of a Whitgift Middle School student, more interested in the excitement of his own developing athletics, and who has now written this story some sixty years later.

In the 1956 Melbourne Olympics, the highs and lows of which I was most keenly aware were those of local distance running star, Gordon Pirie, who had inspired me when he ran seemingly interminable lunchtime laps around my former school field in central Croydon. He twice unsuccessfully battled it out "down under" with Soviet ace Vladimir Kuts, first valiantly in the 10,000m and later 5,000m. In the former, he emerged as the sole challenger for gold, making a race of it until he was eventually destroyed by the relentlessly surging Kuts. Tempered by that experience and amazingly well recovered, he tackled the shorter race more conservatively and was rewarded with the silver medal. The diminutive Derek Johnson also inspired me, when his valiant, but unavailing, bid for 800m victory was thwarted in the final few strides by the stronger and significantly taller American, Tom Courtney. The fortuitous, but nonetheless amazing fourth Olympic high jump appearance by the then 36-year-old Dorothy, twenty years after her first, also failed to catch my attention.

Two more years passed before I eventually became aware of the evergreen Dorothy. No longer involved at international level, but still an enthusiastic competitor, she was a significant scorer for her beloved Mitcham Athletic Club. On 7th April 1958, looking smart and fit, she took part in the 6th Annual Carshalton Trophies Meeting at The Carshalton Arena[1] in South London, and won the long jump. As if not satisfied, she tackled two more events, and also busied herself encouraging and helping other blue and white vested club colleagues. On that day, the author was placed an undistinguished second in the Men's B 440yds in 53.5 seconds!

The success of Dorothy's active career had been prolonged after she, like many South London athletes, sought out the "healing hands" of Worcester Park physiotherapist Ted Chappell[2]. "I only treated her two or three times", he recalled. Such was his diagnostic ability, and so good the subsequent treatment that injured athletes seldom needed to be seen by him for more than the most severe of conditions.

Much of this story emanates from material collected by Dorothy, from her teens to way beyond into her nineties. With

---

1   *Now re-aligned, and renamed The David Weir Centre in recognition of the 2012 Paralympic quadruple gold medallist.*

2   *Ted Chappell was a short-term ice hockey star with Streatham in the immediate post-war years before injury forced him to "change sides" as it were, and he established himself as a highly respected referee. Later almost by accident he took the first steps to becoming one of Britain's pioneering sports physiotherapists. The measure of the man was his range of clients, from the humble club athlete to King Hussein of Jordan and in the upper echelons of athletics Sebastian (now Lord) Coe.*

medals and other memorabilia this developed into what became a veritable Aladdin's Cave. By the time I first saw this archive, it had been clearly well loved but irreverently and haphazardly stashed in sideboard drawers, paper bags and on the floor of her Sanderstead home.

Cracked and faded photographs, torn or dog-eared letters conveying international selection and congratulations, moth-eaten badges, prestigious invitations and menu cards, have all contributed to the astonishing mosaic of recall that this quadruple Olympian has been able to provide. Sadly, this book was begun as Dorothy's health was declining, and it could not be completed before her death.

Dorothy was deservedly lauded for competing at four Olympic Games in which she won two silver medals, as a World Record holder and more recently as a key contributor to her sport as coach, manager and official. She has only been surpassed by Tessa Sanderson, British javelin star of the 1970s and 1980s. Sanderson, unimpeded by war, doubtless benefiting from sophisticated coaching, a more nutritious diet, and not having the challenge of a young family, notched up six Olympic appearances. The thrower also bettered Dorothy in the medal stakes, winning gold in Los Angeles, and matched Dorothy when it came to record breaking.

Dorothy always felt she could and should have done better...

> Had the rules not changed after the 1936 Olympic Games!

> Had her bra strap not broken!

> Had Arthur Wint, the great Jamaican, not fallen near her before a crucial jump!

> Had THAT wasp not stung her just as she was about to compete!

Had not Tom Richards' 1948 marathon finish coincided with the final stages of her high jump!

Had the run up on her side not been wet and slippery!

Who knows, had those things not happened, what further embellishments might there have been to Dorothy's career?

Or, Had she been coached on the more efficient Western Roll sooner!

Regardless, the fascinating story of this great competitor is one steeped in athletics achievement, history and the evolution of the sport.

Dorothy took a keen interest in the compilation of her story, and gave her seal of approval to progressive drafts.

Read on...

Chapter 1
A LITTLE BOUNDER

Elizabeth and Harold Odam were living in Stockwell, South London when, with the assistance of their family doctor, who had to be summoned from church, their daughter was born on 14th March in 1920. The little girl, the third of three children with two older brothers, was christened Dorothy Beatrice Jennie.

The oblivious infant arrived into a London of double-deck omnibuses with external stairs and clanking double-deck trams. Steam trains and household fires belched smoke, blackening buildings all over the city; the coal-merchants of the day, heads protected by suitably sculpted sacks, supplied fuel for millions of households. Together with milkmen, and most other delivery men, they still relied on natural horse power to reach their destinations. It was a dirty, widely deprived and often unpleasant environment.

Father, Harold, a First World War veteran and hero for rescuing a horse in battle, was by then established as an electrical engineer, while mother, Elizabeth, was an accomplished dancer, who had appeared on the same bill as the great Marie Lloyd. One of Elizabeth's party tricks was to perform the splits up a door. Fortunately for Dorothy, her mother's flexibility was clearly conveyed in the genes to her daughter, who later benefited on a very different "stage", the athletics arena.

Young Dorothy's stay in Stockwell was relatively short, with her parents being lured away, allegedly, by the expansive charm of a clearly unscrupulous estate agent. He claimed that the smell of the sea could be experienced at Mitcham just a few miles further south. He might more honestly have advertised the rural charms of the area noted for its many sweet-smelling lavender fields. Today, sadly, the urban sprawl has engulfed all but one remaining beacon of fragrant purple in neighbouring

Carshalton. Not entering the equation then was the fact that the new Odam home was rather too near to the Beddington Sewage Farm for olfactory comfort. With the wind in the wrong quarter, it was notorious for its all too evident "counter attractions".

Number 9 Edenvale Road, was a compact mid-terrace house which did, however, boast many pluses, among which featured the open aspect of the North Mitcham Association tennis courts opposite, and most conveniently a two-lane cinder running path alongside. Naturally her memories of the following few distant years are scant, and maybe thankfully so, for times were hard with World War One and its privations having ground painfully to a halt only two years before her birth. It would not be until the little girl was eight years old that women athletes first competed in track and field events in the Olympic Games. Those Games of 1928 in Amsterdam saw them contesting five events, and the inaugural women's high jump gold was won by Ethel Calderwood of Canada with a clearance of 1.59m.

The uninhibited youngster managed to establish something of a reputation for being adventurous, by climbing trees and for falling into a nearby pond. Fortunately for the sport of athletics, she did not injure herself or develop an alternative liking for swimming, and the rest has become sporting history. During her earliest years while brothers George and Jim were attending nearby Gorringe Park School, Dorothy followed in their educational footsteps at Gorringe Park Infants, where she started at the age of five. She recalled having had to take sandwiches for lunch. Much to her brothers' displeasure they were charged with the responsibility of keeping a watchful eye on their lively young sister en route to school. Understandably, they preferred their own company on the other side of the road! On one occasion this nearly led to her untimely end, for when she dashed across to them without looking, she experienced a near miss with a fast approaching vehicle. With Brighton and the lure of the seaside some fifty miles further south of where they lived, and with father, Harold, a willing driver, Dorothy and her brothers, George and Jim, were often treated to holiday trips to the Sussex coast. There, young legs doubtless benefited from sprinting around on the shingle with youthful disregard and on warm days splashing into the welcoming sea for a swim. Later with her brothers away at boarding school, Dorothy enjoyed much more freedom as the centre of her mother's attention at home. She happily played hop-scotch and skipped a lot at school, which doubtless laid the very foundations for her future as an athlete.

On my recent visit to the former Odam house in Edenvale Road, the bemused Anglo-Jamaican granny with whom I spoke, was much relieved at not being hassled to buy double glazing, and pleased to hear of the world-famous former resident of her son's house. By curious coincidence an elderly lady in an impressive BMW parked nearby not only knew the whereabouts of Gorringe Park School, but knew it personally as a former pupil. Asked if she knew of Dorothy, she revealed that her family had lived a few houses further along the road, and that she and her sister, still resident, had as teenagers been thrilled to have such a notable neighbour. "We were always so excited to see Dorothy, our Olympian, when she went by", she recalled.

Dorothy discovered high jumping in 1931 at the age of eleven, through her astute junior school teacher, Miss Jones, who challenged the sports-minded youngster to "Jump over that rope!"[3], which she duly did with ease. The school mistress must have been impressed for Dorothy was immediately selected to compete in the Mitcham District Schools' Sports, when to the delight of her teacher and her parents, she won and was also awarded the meeting best performance prize.

Dorothy had by then clearly caught the eye of the local athletics cognoscenti, and was offered a scholarship to recently formed Mitcham Athletic Club. This was a significant move, for the club enjoyed all the facilities of the News of the World track near Mitcham Common. Jumping pits apart, these

---

3   In those days children jumped over a rope, weighted at both ends to maintain tension, and landed in a sand pit.

boasted a changing hut, toilet and wash hand basin! Thus started an association which flourished until the 1960s, when her club was controversially assimilated into the new Sutton and District AC, a move many thought politically motivated. Fiercely proud and hugely disappointed at the demise of her beloved club, Dorothy would never become reconciled to the change.

Miss Jones could have hardly realised that her simplistic selection method had launched her protégée on course to what was destined to become one of the most impressive high jump careers in history. During this time, while her father played cricket at Worcester Park, and her mother acted as dutiful scorer, Dorothy was allowed to run footloose and fancy free on the grass nearby. Her best friend then was a girl called Maisie Otto, who was the same age and shared the same birthday. They kept in touch, and until very recently enjoyed an annual reunion.

Once when she was twelve, Dorothy availed herself of the opportunity to take up a sprint challenge from the cosseted daughter of a neighbouring army Major, with a passe-partout set[4] being offered as prize. Even then, competitive through and through, Dorothy prevailed, and her rival wept! In the same year, Dorothy was nominated as reserve for Surrey for the All England Schools Championships which were held at Guildford.

After winning the Surrey Schools junior girls high jump in 1933, the enthusiastic youngster earned county schools selection for the junior girls' high jump at the English Schools Championships which were staged in faraway Southend-on-Sea! There she excelled despite a leg injury, and took second place with a 5' clearance (1.52m – although another source gave her final height cleared as 4' 10", 1.47m).

Leaving school at fourteen as many did way back then, it was deemed prudent for her to sign on at Pitman's Secretarial

---

4   *Picture framing kit*

College to train as a "Temp". Coincidentally, a fellow student was Dorothy Manley who was also destined to become an Olympian and silver medallist. Flexibility in her subsequent employment was seen to be ideal, giving more opportunity to train and to maximise her potential.

Athletically, at fifteen, Dorothy had taken off in more ways than one, winning both the Surrey County and Southern Counties senior high jump titles, peaking with a silver medal spot in the National Championships. This was the last time she was beaten in the National Championships until war intervened in 1939.

While King George V and Queen Mary were celebrating their Silver Jubilee, the attractive teenage Dorothy got her own "royal acclaim". Her upright figure and golden hair clearly caught the eye of the North Mitcham Mayday Festival organisers, and she was crowned the Mitcham May Queen. Dressed in sensational white satin and crimson velvet, she looked totally stunning.

During her formative days as a fast emerging high jumper, Dorothy went on foot to the Mitcham track where she trained enthusiastically, light permitting, on Tuesday and Thursday evenings, and on Sunday mornings. She often had the advantage of being able to watch another Mitcham AC member, Mary Milne, the reigning British champion. The club became one of the strongest women's units at the time, boasting no fewer than twelve internationals.

By this time, the fast emerging Mitcham athlete, who had won 28 trophies, and equalled the world record of 5' 5" (1.65m) indoors during training, declared her achievements as "Not so wonderful!", suggesting that she was focused on far greater things.

Early in 1935, the leggy 15-year-old Dorothy caught the eye of the experts when she finished an impressive runner-up in the WAAA indoor championships at the Wembley Pool. That summer, her first South of England title started an unbeaten run of six and in the WAAA Championships she matched her indoor result by once again finishing runner-up with a clearance of 5' (1.52m) behind Mary Milne who won at 5' 1" (1.55m). Dorothy's winning Southern Counties clearance at Chiswick was 5' 1¾" (1.57m) but she successfully raised the bar to 5' 3" (1.60m) to give a clarion call of her arrival on the scene. Among the sports headlines which followed was "Miss Odam's ambition is to jump higher than her own height – now 5ft 4in".

A few months later, Dorothy further leapt into prominence at Morecambe where she was close to the British record in a four-way tie at 5' 2" (1.57m). She certainly did not conform to the reported "Masculine Girls, strength and sturdiness were the characteristics of the competitors".

In the same year, Dorothy finally beat Mary Milne, the British record holder, who had moved the stagnating event forward from Phyllis Green's British record of 5' 2¼" (1.58m) set in 1927, to 5' 3 ¼" (1.61m).

Apart from the years when she wasn't competing she remained top of the UK high jump rankings until 1949, only to be knocked off her notable perch in 1950 by Sheila Alexander (later Lerwill) whose season's best was 1.69m.

Illustrations 1919 - 1939

Dorothy at the 1936 Berlin Olympic Games, painted by Alice Chandler

Harold and Elizabeth Odam, Dorothy's parents

The Odam family home in Edenvale Road

Dorothy, aged 14, with trophies

Dorothy as May Queen of North Mitcham in 1935

Dorothy, aged 15, with trophies

Mitcham Netball Club 'B' team 1935-6

Mlle Nicolas congratulates Dorothy, Blackpool, June 1936

Dorothy's much cherished 1936 blazer badge

GB Olympians visit to dairy in Berlin, 1936 (Dorothy centre of back row)

Dorothy between jumps, Berlin 1936

Dorothy in Olympics high jump action 1936
(Leni Riefenstahl photo)

Berlin medallists (2nd Dorothy Odam, 1st Ibolya Csak, 3rd
Elfriede Kaun) escorted by Lord Aberdare to podium

On the Berlin podium, 3rd Elfriede Kaun, 1st Ibolya Csak, 2nd Dorothy Odam

Berlin medallists, 1st Ibolya Csak, 3rd Elfriede Kaun, 2nd Dorothy Odam

Dorothy wearing the oak wreath presented to
Berlin medallists

1936 Olympic Second Place Certificate

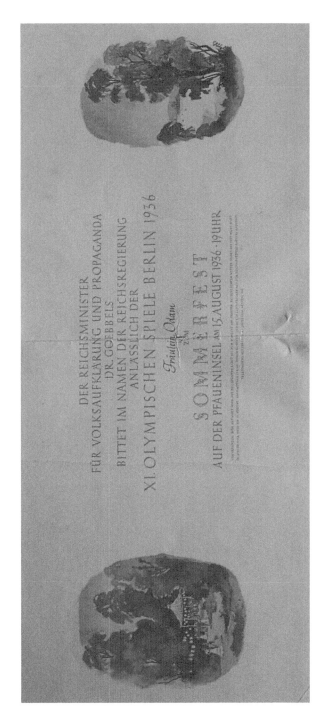

Dorothy's Olympic Party invitation from Dr Goebbels

Dorothy, aged 17 with trophies

Dorothy with Gladys (Sally) Lunn and Dorothy Saunders at
Tilbury going to Empire Games 1938

S.S. Ormonde.

SS Ormonde, the ship that took them to Australia for Empire
Games 1938

When the Orient liner Ormonde called at Gibraltar the British team of athletes travelling to Australia for the Empire Games went ashore for a brief exercise. Here is Miss Dorothy Odam, the high jump champion, practising before members of the Gibraltar garrison.

Press cutting of their stop-off in Gibraltar. Dorothy was experimenting with the Western Roll at this time, without success

Dorothy's World Record Plaque. Record set in 1939, but not recognised until 1957.

Chapter 2
TEENAGE TRIUMPH IN BERLIN.

Throughout the 1930s, a certain "Mister Hitler" was evolving his master plan to dominate the world, and had won the right to stage the 1936 Olympic Games for Germany and the World in Berlin[5]. No effort was spared, nor money held back in the effort to promote Nazi Germany as a major player in sport and a political power not to be taken lightly.

In March 1936, Harold Abrahams[6], reporting on the second indoor championships at Wembley, wrote in the national press

> "The applause that greeted Mrs Dumbrill (Milne) and Miss Odam in the high jump, when after half an hour they tied at 5ft. 2in, was vociferous. Both these ladies should go to Berlin in the Olympic team".

This was the first of her eight Women's AAA high jump titles, her clearance being the highest she was to achieve indoors.

Dorothy laid claim to the British record at Brentwood School on June 1st when she cleared 5' 5" (1.65m) to win her second Southern Women's championship, ahead of one Mary Dumbrill 5' 3" (1.60m) and Dora Greenwood 5' (1.52m). This equalled the then World Record, but for some reason this mark is listed in the IAAF Progression of World Records as unratified.

Curiously, this followed thirteen years after another claimed "world record", also set at Brentwood, by Sophie Elliott-Lynn, a more than imaginative aviatrix. Her supposed height of 4' 10½" (1.485m), set in 1923 and ratified by the FSFI in 1934, has been

---

5   *The games had been awarded to Berlin by the IOC on 13th May 1931, almost 2 years before the Nazi Party took power. To keep the games and avoid a boycott they gave an assurance that there would be no discrimination against Jewish or black athletes.*

6   *Harold Abrahams was Olympic 100m Champion in Paris in 1924, and later featured as co-subject with Eric Liddell in the classic film Chariots of Fire. He became a top British athletics administrator in the 1950s.*

questioned by later research,[7] which has uncovered a result in which Elliott-Lynn was placed second behind Hilda Hatt, both having cleared 4' 10" (1.47m). According to her biography "Lady Icarus", Sophie had written at the time to her Aunt Lou, mentioning that she "...had broken the world high jump record with a clearance of 4' 11" on August 6th. The same source casts further doubt on the claim, stating that the height achieved was ½" shy of 4' 11".

Although still of tender years, Dorothy's emerging talent earned her selection for the England team in an International match against France, Holland, Scotland and Sweden at Stanley Park, Blackpool on 10th June 1936 as part of the town's Jubilee celebrations, and she certainly rose to the occasion. There she shone in the high jump, which she won at 5' 3" (1.60m) before progressing to a fine leap of 5' 4" (1.62m)[8]. One of the world's greatest athletes but yet to set foot on the major stage, Fanny Koen of Holland, tied for third place. This was the first time that Dorothy and Fanny met, and the Dutchwoman's first competition on British soil. The encounter led to the two rivals becoming lifelong friends.

Victory in the outdoor WAAA championships that July clinched Dorothy's selection for Great Britain for the Olympics the next month. The delighted Mitcham girl was unwittingly on the road to an outstanding and fascinating athletics career.

One of Dorothy's greatest thrills after selection, was to show the uniform to her friends, but with athletics and more particularly women's athletics being very low key in the 1930s, it seems that her parents did not let their daughter's youthful fame ruffle the family routine, although Mrs Odam did express her pleasure. Her brothers, Jim and George, both sadly died relatively young and hardly had the opportunity to celebrate

---

7   Brant/Wasco. An earlier performance of 1.50m in Berlin in 1921 by Gertrude Doring of Germany muddies the waters, as does another German Waltraude Schmidt, who jumped the same height in Dresden in the same year.
8   This was given at the time as a British record, casting doubt on the earlier Brentwood mark. There may be good reason why the Brentwood jump was not ratified.

their young sister's talent.

The British Olympic Association Handbook issued to team members contained a congratulatory message from its Patron, His Majesty King Edward VIII, expressing his view that "they would maintain the tradition of British sportsmanship". Also indicative of the times, were such gems as

> "General Equipment. ---- When watching the games women will wear sunburn coloured stockings and white shoes".

> "Food on the journey. --- A ticket for breakfast on the steamer and lunch on the train on the outward journey, also a ticket for dinner on the train and breakfast on the train to London on the homeward journey will be found in your ticket book".

> "The team managers will pay all gratuities which are necessary only on the English trains. The lunch and dinner tickets include the 10% gratuity. Wine, beer and mineral waters must be paid for by the individuals concerned".

> "Return journey. - ensure that berths are booked on the steamer—otherwise it will mean a night on the deck".

The excited young Mitcham athlete's journey to Berlin began at Liverpool Street Station, London at 8.30pm, where she met the eleven other British women athletes (men travelled separately) and three chaperones. It was next stop Harwich, then across the North Sea by ferry from the port of Harwich to The Hook of Holland, and onwards by train, the North German Express, to Berlin Friedrichstrasse Station, arriving at 4.30pm, to conclude an exhausting twenty-hour journey.

Like her team-mates she sported a modest uniform comprising cravat, dress, blazer and a beret. With funds tight, she had made her own shorts and vest, although at least the red, white and blue ribbon for her vest had been provided. Her faithful old spikes, despite sporting a hole, still had to suffice!

As the wide-eyed Britons left their train in the Hauptbahnhof, they thought the "Nice Germans" had laid on a special welcome as an impressive brass band struck up simultaneously. It was only when the Belgian hockey team stepped onto the platform that Dorothy, reassured with her lion mascot, and her colleagues realised that they were being largely disregarded. At least a coach had been laid on for the young women and their team officials to effect safe transit to the physical education college, where they would be housed well away from any British men who might have harboured inappropriate intentions!

The team was treated to their first somewhat daunting taste of Nazi propaganda as they headed through the great German city for their games accommodation at Friedrich Friesen Haus, Reichsportsfeld, Berlin Charlottenberg IX and were driven down streets bedecked with hundreds of huge red and white banners, and emblazoned with Hitler's sinister black swastika.

The politically uninformed teenager had a further rude awakening, as hundreds of Hitler Youth members marched about proudly swinging their swastika armbands, many with shovels and brooms at the slope on their shoulders.

Once installed, and largely undaunted by the overt propaganda, the athletes from forty-nine nations, among them Dorothy and her friends Barbara Burke and Kath Tiffin, set out to explore. On one such sortie, the British girls went into an interesting looking shop and were greeted by the owner, clearly toeing the Party line, with a straight-armed Nazi salute.

"Heil Hitler", he greeted. After a brief discussion the girls unanimously agreed to respond only as they felt they might with a synchronised chorus and a British salute - "Heil King George", they trilled, touching their forelocks simultaneously.

Dorothy was adamant that the magazine "The Oldie" misquoted

her as saying that the response was in part German, accompanied by a girl-guide salute! The timing of the "Heil King George" response is in doubt since the uncrowned Edward VIII did not abdicate until 10th December 1936, and his brother King George VI was not crowned until 15th May 1937. Who is to be believed – Dorothy's memory after more than 70 years may cast some doubt on her more recent recall, but on the other hand the wide use of journalistic licence is common knowledge.[9]

The daily awakening in the females' accommodation in the Friedrich Friesen Haus, which after the Games became the Reich Academy of Physical Culture, was more often than not to the sound of marching feet, adding to the politically charged environment in which the teenager and her team mates found themselves. Looking from her window, Dorothy discovered that the marchers were the aforementioned members of the Nazi Youth Organisation again carrying their unconventional weapons.

This accommodation suited the athletes well, for it was within walking distance of the stadium, but not so their team managers who had to contend with extra distance to the Headquarters at the Village at Doberitz, sixteen miles from the Brandenburg Gate, and eleven from the stadium.

The self-interest of the girls' chaperones housed elsewhere, would later give the girls some measure of freedom, and Dorothy was certainly not slow to take advantage of such lassitude.

With her event one of the last in the athletics programme, Dorothy clearly capitalised on training opportunities to meet athletes from other countries. Still with a twinkle in her eye, she recalled having caught the attention of a "rather good looking" Danish male high jumper at training. The identity of our attractive young Olympian's beau has been lost in the mists

---

9   *It is more likely to have been during a later visit to Germany in 1937 or 1939.*

of distant memory, but one might speculate that the astute Dane was high jumper Poul Otto[10], who made the qualifying standard of 1.85m. The event was won by Cornelius Johnson U.S.A. with 2.03m using the Western Roll technique, which impressed the young Briton who rued the fact that no coach had been on hand in England to teach it to her. Later, the "rather good looking" Dane invited the youngster out, only to be faced with the prospect of "entertaining" all the other British girls, as decreed by the belatedly eagle-eyed chaperones who added that they too would be in attendance!

Defence against inappropriate social interface was clearly deemed more important to be protected from than injury or loss of form. Neither physiotherapists nor coaches featured with the team.

In the Berlin hostel, Dorothy's modest suburban upbringing stood her in very good stead, for she found the food generally acceptable, while many of the more fortunate Americans and Australians were regularly to be heard complaining about their meals.

The arrival of the Fuhrer for the Opening Ceremony predictably generated mass hysteria which was clearly heard some way distant on the polo ground where the athletes were held, pending their parade. They were largely unprotected from the sun for three or so hours, but were at least provided with water to ease their discomfort.

On entering the stadium, the athletes were stunned not only by the mighty roar of the crowd, but also the deafening discharges of numerous cannons, plus the awesome sight of 20,000 symbolic pigeons delightedly celebrating their freedom from the previously mysterious baskets which were spaced around the stadium.

---

10 One can further speculate, that the discerning Dane might have been related to her
   lifelong friend Maisie Otto!

Richard Strauss's Olympic hymn was sung with great gusto, and the Olympic flame, which had originated at Mount Olympus, was greeted with all-embracing emotion as a handsome Aryan torch bearer entered the stadium on his legendary lap to conclude the inaugural torch relay.

It says a great deal for the composure of the young scissor-jumping teenager from Mitcham, that on August 9th 1936, the final day of athletics competition, she was able to control her nerves in a cauldron of 80,000 predominantly Nazi-indoctrinated spectators, all cheering their high jump heroine Elfriede Kaun to success.

Watched by the Nazi leaders, the event lasted for three enthralling hours, during which time the German girls were significantly brought water, but their rivals deprived. Five competitors progressed to attempt 1.60m, Dora Ratjen and Elfriede Kaun of Germany, Marguerite Nicolas of France, Ibolya Csak of Hungary and Dorothy. Dorothy cleared at the first attempt. The others failed. Csak made it on her second attempt and it was not until her third, that the German Kaun succeeded.

The next height, 1.62m, saw further drama with all three competitors failing three times. Under current rules, Dorothy, who had cleared at her first attempt, would have topped the podium, but with the rules of the day the girls were obliged to take part in a jump off. The bar was re-set at 1.62m - the height at which they had all failed. Csak soared clear while the other two failed. The bar was then lowered to 1.60m at which height Dorothy succeeded to win the silver medal. Thus gold and silver medals were decided and Dorothy having cleared the same height as the winner had to settle for second place and Elfriede Kaun took the bronze.

Further still down the field in sixth place was F E Koen of the Netherlands, another of the world's outstanding female Olympians, who, when married, became a global figure as Fanny Blankers-Koen.

1936 Berlin Olympics programme cover for Dorothy's day of competition.
(Courtesy Olympic Studies Centre, Lausanne)

There had been controversy over the German, Gretel Bergmann, a Jewess who having returned from the relative safety of England where her father sent her in 1934, had not been allowed to compete in the German Championships. As a sop to the Americans, she was, however, allowed in 3 other trials in 1935 all of which she won, but with a best of only 1.55m.

In 1936, she was only placed joint third in the German Olympic Trial, and the German authorities nominated a number of competitions where jumpers could prove their performance. In one of these, Gretel Bergmann won and equalled the German record of 1.60m. Her subsequent exclusion from the Games was "explained" as being due to the "mediocre" level of her performance. The German team was not announced until the Americans were already aboard their ship en route to Germany, and it was clear that the whole selection process was something of a charade and the Germans had never intended to select any Jewish athletes. One of the two selected German jumpers was a rather suspiciously deep voiced "woman" Dora Ratjen, of whom we'll hear more later. The women's high jump thus became the only event in which the Germans failed to field three athletes.[11] Gretel later emigrated to the USA where she competed under her new name of Margaret Lambert and ultimately became American high jump champion.

In the Official British Olympic Report, Dorothy's epic is recorded as follows

> "The high jump was the cause for considerable optimism, and when Miss Odam cleared the bar at 5' 3", while both the German and the Hungarian failed at their first attempt, it looked as if there was good reason for our optimism. The Hungarian, however, cleared 5' 3", with her second attempt; the German at the third. The bar was then raised to 5' 3¾", and all three competitors failed,

---

11 *Disproving the myth, put out by American media, that Bergmann was replaced by Ratjen. Ratjen was always going to be selected.*

and the German Kaun failed rather badly".

There was then a first jump-off at 1.62m involving the three of them, where only Csak jumped clear.[12]

> "Csak was declared the winner and the bar was then lowered to 5ft. 3in again. Odam cleared the first time in good style, and Kaun failed. They gave the English girl second place".

The result in the 1936 BOA report had the following comment appended.

> "This provided keen competition among 17 competitors. Miss Odam tied with Miss Csak and Miss Kaun, and in the first jump off Miss Csak won. Miss Odam subsequently beat Miss Kaun for second place. Miss Odam certainly excelled herself and with a little luck might have been our first woman champion in the athletic section of the Olympic Games".

In addition to her well-earned silver medal, Dorothy had a wreath placed on her head. Dorothy recalled it as a "rusty old piece of metal" that ended up in the Tyler dustbin, but this was clearly her memory playing tricks again, as the International Studies Centre in Lausanne has confirmed that all medallists were presented with oak wreaths by the girl members of the Honorary Youth Service.[13] A further impressive award was a plinth-mounted statuette of a black eagle, which avoided the ignominy of the dustbin and remained on display for many years.

Two days after the epic women's high jump competition, Harold Abrahams attended a meeting of the International

---

12 It is frequently said that Ibolya Csak was herself Jewish. However sources connected to her family deny this.
13 Had she won, Dorothy would have been presented with an oak sapling to be planted in her native town. Sadly few of these "Hitler Oaks" now survive, either because of their connection with the Nazi regime or just the ravages of time.

Amateur Athletic Federation at which the rule concerning ties was altered. Had such legislation been in force 48 hours earlier, Dorothy Odam would have been the first British female Olympic athletics champion.

Mischievously, she recalled that she often heard a "man's voice behind", only to find that on turning, doubtless in the hope of having eluded the chaperones' surveillance, that it emanated from a "female" sprinter. Dorothy remained adamant that the first three in the women's 100m were indeed men. There were no sex tests in those distant days, and Dorothy's suspicions appear to have more than a small element of truth. The race was won by Helen Stephens of USA, but the supporters of second placed Stanislawa Walasiewicz were not happy, saying that deep-voiced Stephens was too fast to be a woman, and they demanded that she be given a sex test. Stephens was pronounced to be a woman and the result stood, but the story doesn't end there. Walasiewicz had been born in Poland before her parents decided to emigrate to the USA, where she competed as Stella Walsh. She had decided to compete for her native country, winning gold in 1932 and the silver in 1936, but later went back to America. Then in 1980 she was killed by a stray bullet during an attempted armed robbery, and her autopsy showed that she was intersex, with partially developed male genitalia. There were also serious doubts about Kathe Krauss of Germany, who took the bronze medal.

Dorothy, while confident in competition, was still very much the wide-eyed teenager. As she later recalled, she took a while to pluck up the courage to ask super star Jesse Owens for his autograph. "Aw shucks" he replied "let me get my shoes on first".

The chaperones continued to hold their charges on a tight rein throughout, even trying to debar their athletes from going into a Jewish owned shop. Regardless, they entered, only for Dorothy to be asked to pass on a document revealing the horrors of concentration camps. Unnerved, she showed it to a chaperone who took it away.

An invitation from Dr Goebbels to the post-games Celebration Ball[14] on Pfaueninsel provided a further huge thrill for the wide-eyed teenager, but who, 75 years later and fully conversant with the aforementioned notorious Nazi's crimes during World War 2, still experienced shivers down the spine.

Regardless of such sinister undertones at the time, the ball had an air of magic about it. Dorothy remembers the handsome soldiers lining the pontoon bridge which accessed the venue. She also recalls that in addition to the welcoming Hitler and the somewhat over-attentive Dr Goebbels, many European leaders were also in attendance.

Another lasting non-athletic event that was still firmly etched in the Mitcham girl's memory many years later is a haunting one of the huge airship Hindenburg, the pride of Nazi dirigibles[15], which circled the skies over Berlin for the duration of the Games, often casting its sinister shadow below.

On the human front, and one might reasonably ask, if human is the right word, the relationship between the athletes and their chaperones still rankles. Dorothy has never forgotten the comment of one such woman, when shortly after her high jump success she proudly went into the athletes' dining room understandably expecting praise, only to find herself surprised by her deflating welcome "Miss Odam, you should remember that you are not the only one to win a medal".

It beggars belief that a great achievement by a sixteen year old should have been treated so dismissively. Seldom around to help, and giving little encouragement these dour women officials were more intent on shopping than helping their young Olympic charges.

---

14 *The invitation labeled the occasion a Sommerfest, but Dorothy remembered it as a ball. Dorothy remembered it as being at Schwanenwerder on Wannsee, which is where Goebbels had his villa, but the invitation gives nearby Pfaueninsel (Peacock Island) on the River Havel as the venue.*
15 *The hydrogen filled Hindenburg tragically caught fire in America the following year. This was the end of airships for many decades - Britain had abandoned its own after the R101 disaster.*

The politics surrounding Dorothy's event and other experiences have historically paled into relative insignificance, when compared with the epic white versus black confrontation which Hitler and his lackeys had reportedly built up around the men's long jump and the rivalry between his great blonde Aryan hope, Lutz Long, and the wonderful black American, Jesse Owens. Long was eclipsed by the multi-talented American, but took his defeat like a true sportsman exchanging a friendly handshake with the victor. It was later reported that the sportsman-like German had advised Owens to lengthen his run-up to avoid over stepping the take-off board. Although it has been widely reported that a furious scowling Fuhrer stormed out of the stadium, there are other versions.[16] Happily, well over half a century later, the daughters of the two legendary long jumpers met to recall the great Olympic battle between their respective fathers.

Dorothy's return home to Mitcham was far from heralded by ticker tape or blue and white balloons. The Olympics, it seems, were no big deal in London's suburbs in those austere days. There was little public awareness and hardly any press coverage. On the credit side Mitcham A.C. officials were up to speed with the significance of Dorothy's achievement, and formally recognised it by making the sixteen year old possibly the youngest Life Member of any sporting organisation. The girl also received "stacks of congratulatory letters from kind club members". Mr W G Bateman, the club's Hon. Gen. Secretary, wrote "I was instructed to convey to you the Committee's appreciation of your performances in the Olympics and in Cologne. We all feel that you kept the Mitcham A.C. flag flying in Germany and hope that you will continue with your successes". After the excitement of an Olympic year and her astonishing success in Berlin, Dorothy appears to have made a comfortable return to the domestic scene.

---

16 It has been claimed by several people, German and British that Hitler did shake Owens' hand but the truth was suppressed to paint Hitler in a bad light. Whether or not they shook hands, it is certainly true that Jesse Owens was not treated well on his return to a racially segregated USA.

In 1937 Dorothy took the first of her 3 Surrey high jump titles. She won the event with a clearance of 5' 4" (1.62m). This constituted a championship best performance, a feat which she astonishingly equalled fourteen years later. She then won the second of her outdoor WAAA titles at 1.63m[17], and was similarly successful indoors at 5' 2" (1.59m). Dorothy also made three international appearances, two in Germany with a winning clearance of 1.62m in Wuppertal, and a centimetre lower in Krefeld, finishing 2nd with a clearance of 1.61m behind Dora Ratjen, who equalled the world record and another in Brussels at 1.61m.

Towards the end of 1937 she earned England selection for the British Empire Games to be held in Sydney, Australia, in February 1938. Dorothy conceded that she could not have gone then had it not been for the support of her parents. She even sacrificed her secretarial job into the bargain.

Together with 100 other athletes representing the "Old Country", Dorothy enjoyed a wonderful send off from St Pancras and later the port of Tilbury in the Thames estuary, from where the British teams sailed before Christmas aboard the Orient Liner Ormonde[18] bound for the antipodes. The athletes received greetings from the President of the Empire Games Federation, Sir James Leigh-Wood and Lady Leigh-Wood which included the intriguing phrase "Sir James trusts he will not be misunderstood when he expresses the hope that all concerned will go slow so as not to impair their training in view of the serious work ahead".

Present-day international athletes would not even expect to cross the Channel by ferry to compete in France. It has been claimed that two of the England rowers Basil Beazley and John "Jan" Sturrock were at work on board as ship's engineers[19], before representing England with distinction in the rowing

---

17 From 1933 until 1951 the WAAA championships were metric, apart from the 1 mile race.
18 The Ormonde weighed 14982 tons and had been built at Strathclyde in 1917. She could cruise at 18 knots (21 mph) and was eventually scrapped in 1952.
19 Possibly they were members of the naval reserve in the period leading up to the war.

eight, which beat the Australian crew to gold by ¾ of a length. Imagine more recent heroes Sir Matthew Pinsent and Sir Steve Redgrave even travelling to their Olympics just for a relatively few hours as flight engineers!

Athletics writer Joe Binks (ex-holder of the Mile Record) reported from on board ship to the News of the World. His first report of the great sporting adventure started.....

> "BRITAIN'S ATHLETES LEAVE. GREAT SEND OFF TO AUSTRALIA.
> CONFIDENCE OF THE EMPIRE GAMES PARTY
>
> In the Orient liner Ormonde, at sea Saturday. We have started our great trip to Australia....from time to time I shall tell "News of the World" readers all about the incidents during the trip, and when we land what these fine men and women....are doing in the Games..."..

Binks further wrote

> "There is no doubt about the enthusiasm of these English, Scottish, Welsh and Northern Ireland teams who are singing tonight as the liner ploughs its way out of the English Channel"

The photographs of the departing team show Dorothy carrying a mascot named Harold after her father. After the war this was replaced by "Pest", her beloved lion mascot. It is believed to have come from Budapest, hence the name, and may have been given to her by an admirer. Pest eventually disappeared, to be happily replaced by "Pest 2", bought by her son Barry after a family visit to Hungary in 2007.

Binks' foreboding that a stop at Gibraltar would be insufficient for a warming-up spin was later disproved by Dorothy, who is pictured jumping[20] in front of an admiring audience from the garrison. He added that the athletes would be training every day and that "Early to bed and early to rise rules will have to be observed".

Together with other athletes aged 17 or under, she was confined to ship during the Adelaide stop because of an epidemic of infantile paralysis.

The long voyage indeed proved very worthwhile for Dorothy, who won the Empire title with a clearance of 5' 3" (1.60m) ahead of team mate Dora Gardener (Middlesex Ladies AC), who also cleared 5' 3". It was thanks to these two, and long jump silver medallist Ethel Raby, who leapt 18' 6¾" (5.66m), that the highly-rated, formerly dominant English women were saved the embarrassment of a medal whitewash.

Later, Dorothy ran into trouble when she accompanied her friend and team mate, Margaret Holloway, on a post-competition visit from their base at the Kirketon Private Hotel to the Canadian quarters, at the invitation of the former's new found beau. Unfortunately for them, this apparently innocent liaison led them to an exuberant, slightly late and chatty return to "English soil". This enraged the dour team manager, Mrs Grimes, who was waiting in Dorothy's room, ready to give the miscreants a dressing down.

Commenting on her Games success, Dorothy reported that her efforts had been hampered by a strong wind, which stopped her setting a new world record. "I was jumping well and went straight up to 5' 3". I feel sure I should have done it, but a terrific wind blew up", she complained. Tom Lavery[21] with the same wind behind him, bettered the Games 120yds high hurdles record, but his time was disallowed on account of the

---

20 The picture shows Dorothy doing a Western Roll. Her son, Barry, confirms she was experimenting with the Western Roll technique before the war, but without a coach she couldn't jump as high as with Scissors.
21 Thomas Lavery was a South African athlete born in Scotland in 1911. He won the gold medal in the 120yds hurdles in Sydney in 1938 and also won bronze in Auckland in 1950

assistance.

After the Games, Dorothy set a Western Australian record of 5' 3" (1.60m) in Perth. Until 1948 the British record could be set by any athlete competing in Britain, and presumably Australia had similar rules.

Dorothy memorably celebrated her 18th birthday, 14th March, at sea shortly after leaving Colombo on the return voyage aboard the RMS Stratheden[22], and "the team gave a bumper party in her honour". There was further adventure when the ship ran aground on a sandbank in the Suez Canal, but she was re-floated after eight hours, giving the athletes time for "shore leave" at Port Said for some shopping. Despite their disembarkation at 2am the shops were open thanks to the ever alert Egyptians who were always ready to take the travellers' money!

On returning home, Dorothy told the local press that
"It had been a wonderful trip...wherever we went we were treated like celebrities...on the outward journey, Christmas Day was the most remarkable I have ever spent. We were in Colombo in scorching heat with dinner at the Galle Face Hotel. ... while in Australia, some of the men met Don Bradman[23], and we broadcast several times on the radio, each team singing national songs"

Sometime later, and with the dust seemingly having settled, the aforementioned "unfortunate incident" was followed up by a meeting at the England Empire Games office. Dorothy, with her mother alongside, was further reprimanded and advised to exercise greater maturity in the future. Dorothy blames the post-Sydney incident for subsequent international omissions,

---

22 *RMS Stratheden was built by Vickers Armstrong and launched on 10 June 1937. She was 23700 tons gross. Her last voyage from Australia was on 15th September 1963 having completed 55 round trips. She was sold to J S Latsis of Athens and given a new name before being eventually broken up in 1969.*
23 *Donald Bradman, one of the greatest Australian cricketers ever, who was smilingly pictured on the back cover of the Games programme advertising Peters Ice Cream "Two Australian Champions". He was knighted eleven years later.*

including the European Championships in Vienna.

Early in 1939 she emphatically etched her name in athletics history, when she became the third Briton, and the thirteenth female to set a new world high jump record since official records started in 1922. On Whitsun Bank Holiday Monday, May 29th 1939, Brentwood witnessed its second world high jump record when Dorothy cleared 1.66m on her second attempt to retain the South of England Championship for the 5th time, with Doris Endreweit a distant second (1.55m). The event was one of the star attractions incorporated in a predominantly local carnival style programme for the Brentwood Hospital Sports on the clearly popular Brentwood School Playing Field. Dorothy's performance there, achieved using the favoured but uneconomical scissors style, saw her beat Mitcham AC colleague Mary Dumbrill too.

With prizes on offer in the open events, Dorothy, ever the young opportunist, seized her chance and took a productive second in the women's handicap high jump, in which, competing most likely off scratch, she couldn't match the 5' 7" (including a handicap of +6") achieved by Alice Flack! The canteen of cutlery which she won that day remained much prized, and was still on show for all to see in her display cabinet right until she moved into a nursing home in 2014.

The Chelmsford Chronicle of June 9th reported that "Prizes were presented by Mrs J F F Lawrence of Pilgrims Hall …..There was an excellent gate in spite of the cold weather…..and due to many entries the programme took an extra hour to complete".

No mention of a world record! Well there were numerous other attractions that clearly caught the eye of a non-athletics-aware reporter most likely sent along on unwelcome holiday duty. To relate more to the time of Dorothy's achievement, it is worth recording that alongside the athletics report in a local newspaper, a Ford advertisement featured new tractors from £150 and new vans and cars from £100.

At the time, Dorothy's jump of 1.66m was not recognised as a world record, as in the previous year the deep-voiced German Ratjen (whom she had always believed to be a man) had cleared 1.70m in Vienna. A few days after that performance in the European Championships, Ratjen's cover had been blown when the masquerading athlete was apprehended on the Vienna to Cologne Express at Magdeburg station. An astute ticket inspector, suspicious of the individual's hairy hands, called police Detective Sergeant Sommering who was not fooled by the ID presented. The story goes that, determined to discover whether this was really a man, he threatened an examination...

"If I resist?" Ratjen queried.

"Then you would be guilty of obstruction", the detective responded.

After a moment of hesitation, the questionable athlete capitulated, confessing to indeed being a man.

The life of "man-woman" Dora Ratjen thus ceased on 21st September 1938 and that of Heinrich Ratjen began. The subject of so much sporting intrigue lived on until 22nd April 2008 and now lies buried in a Bremen cemetery.

The German authorities later confirmed that Ratjen was in fact a hermaphrodite. It is doubtful whether the Reich was involved in the deception as Ratjen had been registered as a girl at birth and brought up as a girl. Over the years, Ratjen realised he was male but continued to live as a female. Much of the confusion about the story (including the name Hermann Ratjen) came from a film, "Berlin 36", itself based on a Time article that rewrote much of the history.[24]

---

24 Lest any British reader be lured into a feeling of superiority, it should be pointed out that two winners of WAAA championships in the inter-war period later fathered children. The problem of "intersex" athletes and who is a woman has long dogged sport and continues to do so. This did not stop British newspapers saying things such as "unfair to have the English girls compete against freaks".

Ratjen's World Record remained in the record books until the DRL (German Athletic Authority) advised the IAAF of the situation, and, in addition, the unfortunate person's European title was rescinded. It was further decreed there would be no further mention of the saga in public. Ratjen then requested a name change to Heinrich, which was duly registered.

Happily for Dorothy with the issue resolved, her own world record eventually stood, although it took many years before it was officially confirmed.

In late July 1939, Dorothy, blissfully unaware of the gathering clouds of war, competed in what for her and all other top athletes transpired to be the last international contest for seven years. One of a modest contingent of "Brits", and small teams from several other countries, she travelled once more to Nazi Germany for a meeting billed as an Olympic Trial (Olympisher Prufungskampfe) event, promoted by the ISTAF[25] in the Berlin Olympic Stadium.

Also involved were athletes from the top German clubs of Charlottenburg, Dresden and Potsdam. There was certainly no sign of the impending World War 2 on the happy faces of the fraternising athletes and officials who featured in photographs taken in the days leading up to the competition.

Dorothy was in good form, winning the high jump and missing her own world record by one centimetre. Her best leap of 1.65m saw her in a class of her own, ahead of five others including fellow Briton, Dora Gardner, who was placed 4th, 10cm below her compatriot. Two Germans, Feodora Zu Solms (MTV Wunsdorf) and Elfriede Kaun (Kieler TV) were both 2 cm adrift in 2nd and 3rd places. The final place in the small field went to yet another German, Erika Eckel (TV 79 Munchen).

Leichtathletik Magazine reported that, "........The two German

---

25 ISTF Internationale Stadionfest was promoted under the auspices of NSRL the German national sports body which Adolf Hitler had placed under Nazi control the previous year. The event has, in happier recent times, been embraced by the IAAF as one of its annual world challenge events.

women were behind the English girl, Odam, who can be expected to produce world record breaking jumps soon".

The German hosts did, however, achieve significant success that weekend when Christel Schultz won the women's long jump with a world record distance of 6.12m. Fanny Koen (Netherlands) who came second, became the next world record holder when as Fanny Blankers-Koen she improved to 6.25m.

Any aspirations for the 1940 Tokyo-hosted summer Olympic Games were soon to disappear, with Japan involved in an aggressive war with China that would soon spread. A hastily arranged transfer to Helsinki also bit the dust as German aggression in Europe, with their march into Poland on 1st September 1939, prompted the start of six years of terrible hostilities. Two days later the United Kingdom and France declared war on Germany.

Briefly back for routine training at The News of the World track in Mitcham, the attractive young high jumper had caught the eye of quarter miler, Dick Tyler, who made sure he secured a place on the club's day out to Brighton. He then cunningly contrived to follow Dorothy directly on to the coach and sit down beside the unwitting girl! Ever the gentleman, Dick recalled that he was "well behaved and discreet" throughout the trip. The chemistry soon became two-way, with Dorothy later claiming that she chased Dick around the Mitcham track area with a javelin!

The pair were clearly destined for each other, and became engaged following a purposeful visit by Dick to the Odam's home. The couple were happily married at St Barnabas Church, Mitcham on April 27th 1940.

Illustrations 1940 - 1957

Picture of Dorothy that Dick carried in his tank through
the war. Note the scorch marks.

Dick Tyler watching Dorothy playing the piano

Dick and Dorothy's wedding

Dorothy's Physical Training course 1943, with Dorothy 4th from left in 2nd row

Detail from the PT course, showing Dorothy's hair style

RAF Ruislip Netball team 1943-4

Cartoon of Dorothy the Netball player

Dorothy jumping over Barry's pram with David alongside.

Rare, but fuzzy, picture of Dorothy at 1948 London Olympics

Arthur Wint's hamstring injury makes him fall into high jump area: a distraction for Dorothy.

Tom Richards, silver medallist in marathon: another
distraction for Dorothy
(Photo from Tom Richards Jnr)

Evidence that Dorothy left the high jump to cheer
Tom Richards

Dorothy getting her silver medal on the 1948 London Olympic women's high jump podium, 2nd Dorothy Tyler, 1st Alice Coachman, 3rd Micheline Ostermeyer

Mrs. D. J. Tyler, British girl who was second in the high jump, gets a kiss from the winner, Miss A. Coachman, of U S A.

Vanquished and Victor. Dorothy receiving a consolation kiss from Alice Coachman

Scarf showing first 6 in each event at 1948 London Olympics.

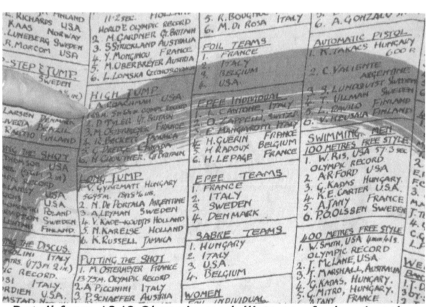

Detail from 1948 Olympic medallists scarf, showing the women's high jump. Note - should be B Crowther

Sequence showing Western Roll jump. At Tooting Bec track
1949

Tilbury Dockside before boarding the Tamaroa to go to New Zealand for the 1950 Empire Games. L to R Jean Desforges, Dorothy Manley, Margaret Walker, Elizabeth Church, Margaret Wellington, Lilian Preece, Sylvia Cheeseman, Doris Batter, Dorothy Tyler

SS Tamaroa

Podium at 1950 European championships. 2nd Dorothy Tyler, 1st Sheila Alexander, 3rd Galina Ganeker

Training at Mitcham with News of the World Shed in the background

Her admiring sons watch Dorothy jumping

Winning Surrey long jump at Wimbledon Speedway Stadium 1951 (Dorothy's personal favourite action shot)

Hurdles training at White City. Dorothy noted that she had to pay one shilling admission

Hurdling against a man during the Festival of Britain 1951

Practising the javelin, circa 1951

The Mitcham AC team winners of Atalanta Trophy, Portsmouth 1951. Dorothy standing far right.

Dorothy with team colleague and rival Sheila Lerwill at
Eccleston Square en route to Helsinki for the 1952 Olympics
(PA Photo)

Part of the Great Britain 1952 Olympic team ready for
departure, Dorothy at back just right of centre

Dorothy jumping in Helsinki in the 1952 Olympics, where she
took 7th equal place. (PA Photo)

The medal winners in the high jump at the 1954 Empire and Commonwealth Games in Vancouver. L to R 3rd Alice Whitty, 2nd Dorothy Tyler, 1st Thelma Hopkins

Dorothy jumping in 1956 Olympics
(Victoria Public Records Photo, courtesy Trevor Vincent)

Dorothy pictured with part of ever-increasing trophy haul, Circa 1957

Dorothy's collection of badges and pennants

Chapter 3
SERVING KING AND COUNTRY

With the declaration of War, athletics in the United Kingdom and in all non-neutral nations quickly went on the back-burner.

Following the German bombing of the family home, Dorothy's mother persuaded her to evacuate to the safety of Wales to stay with a hitherto unknown family. Dorothy stayed a while but then felt duty bound to return and join the WAAF as an HGV driver instead. The dutiful Dorothy found herself serving king and country at her first posting, RAF Watton in Suffolk, later moving to RAF Scampton, home of 617 Squadron, the renowned Dambusters[26]. The resourceful teenager fully availed herself, duties permitting, of all sporting opportunities, also qualifying as a PTI (Physical Training Instructor), which brought her into direct contact with several of the heroic airmen, and which also turned out to prove of value some 20 years later, allowing her to become a PE teacher. It was hardly surprising that she continued to shine, successfully taking several station athletics titles, as well as playing hockey, netball and cricket with sport still playing an important part in her life during the war. Most of her athletics prizes were torches, which she often recalled with some scorn.

Dick was by then posted to the western desert, to the Tobruk theatre in North Africa where he served with distinction in the tank regiment equipped with Sherman "Honeys", which with others ensured the taking of the city. If that experience had not been enough, his regiment was then posted to Burma where, after a serious action with the Japanese, their tanks ran out of fuel, and they were forced into a week-long 150-mile trek out of Burma. At that time Dick was reported to have gone missing. He had collapsed with jaundice and it was only thanks

---

26 *Stars of a famous film, this squadron crippled the German industrial war effort by breaching key dams with the innovative "Bouncing Bombs", the brainchild of inventor Barnes Wallis.*

to the care and loyalty of his local guide that he eventually made it back to India. Once in relative safety there, he and his commissioned colleagues were put up in Government House, where they "recharged their human batteries" before being shipped back to the western desert.

Very little else has emerged of Dorothy's wartime sporting exploits beyond the solid recollection of a fellow Olympian suffering one surprise defeat in a high jump competition when beaten by Cicely Myall, an army rival and member of Spartan Ladies AC.

Dick and Dorothy were separated for the duration of the war. Despite not seeing each other, a constant flow of letters between them kept their flame of devotion burning brightly, with Dorothy affectionately addressed by Dick as "My Gloriana".

Picking up the pieces together with the rest of Britain's relieved but war-wearied population, the couple re-started life together as soon as they could following demobilisation and with nowhere else to go, settled in at the old Odam family Edenvale Road home with Elizabeth, Dorothy's mother. Dick and Dorothy stayed briefly in a flat in nearby Thornton Heath, soon to return to Edenvale Road where mother Odam willingly provided vital care for the boys. They remained there until 1957, when they moved to their new home in Ballards Way, South Croydon, incorporating a flat for the ageing Mrs Odam.

They had emerged into a London of shortages and rationing. The old red buses, emblazoned in gold with the words 'London Transport' and sporting external staircases along with the smoke-belching steam trains, which had survived the Nazi bombing, had now been returned to full civilian service. The city's roads were once again brightened at night by street lighting that had been switched off during the war. The beams of car headlights were once again obvious, having been compulsorily dipped and minimised from 1939 to 1945.

After two war-enforced absences in 1940 and 1944, the rebirth of the Olympic Games was agreed for 1948 and the British offer to host in London and Torbay was duly accepted by the International Olympic Committee. Meanwhile, Dorothy's high jumping career was modestly re-launched in the WAAA Championships staged at the Tooting Bec track on August 18th 1945, when she took the silver medal, clearing 5' 0" (1.52m), the same height as achieved by event winner, Dora Gardener, of Middlesex Ladies.

Their first son, David, was born on 2nd May 1946, but later that year Dorothy was jumping again, clearing 5' 0" (1.52m) on 17 August in London. Second son, Barry, was born on 21st October 1947. The new mother was short of competition, but the prospect of the London Olympic Games, to be staged at the Wembley Stadium in 1948, provided her with the perfect stimulus to get the show on the road again.

With the bottled-up athlete in her champing at the bit, Dorothy's sole sporting aim was to win selection for the fast approaching Games. She quickly resumed serious training with Barry just a month old, and returned to competition seven months later. This would have been impossible without the unstinting support of the devoted Dick and her mother.

Initially not even listed among the "Probables" for the 1948 Olympics, Dorothy had to wait for selection and its associated benefits. Among these were food parcels, some of which came from the sympathetic Australian government, to help their undernourished Commonwealth colleagues!

Dorothy recalled that life then was tough, with food remaining rationed, although once selected as a games probable, she received extra rations, mainly meat, which when collected by Dick was, more often than not, generously over the ration for his athlete wife. Fellow Olympian, 1500m runner Bill Nankeville, substantiates those difficult times with a "Dad's Army"-like memory of how he charmed somewhat more than his fair meat ration out of his sympathetic butcher!

Top British Official Jack Crump remembering her achievement as a 16 year old, twelve years earlier, speculated, "Wouldn't it be wonderful, if she could produce a similar success in London?" Little did he realise that the determined south Londoner would do just that and a great deal more in the years to come.

Then aged 28, Dorothy still had the memory of her Berlin Olympic frustration twelve years before. She re-focused on the London Games, while the host city was still rebuilding after its war-time pounding.

So there then began an even greater interest in Dorothy, the mother and potential double Olympian. Press photographers were almost falling over themselves to snap the perfect picture. One in particular was memorable, showing her clearing a suitably safe low line of nappies in the back garden, complete with offspring and pram in the background.

There was no major new building for the games, although a running track plus field event facilities had to be installed at the Wembley Stadium, while the 450m velodrome at Herne Hill was resurfaced to ensure safe cycling contests. The former was completed just two weeks before the games opened.

London's offer to host the first games for twelve years, often dubbed "The Austerity Olympics", provided Dorothy, now Odam-Tyler and "no longer a lanky schoolgirl", with her second major international stage, and conveniently not so far from home. With her second son, Barry, just six months old Dorothy's preparations were, of necessity, centred on training with Mitcham AC, while other aspirants languished in the relative luxury of the Butlin's Holiday Camp at Clacton-on-Sea!

Her high jumping was unsophisticated to say the least. Approaches were not set in tablets of stone, "just nine or so strides", she said, while her landings into sand might not have been considered to be safe by the deep foam module cosseted exponents of the present day. She trained irregularly, but progressed well and avoided injury, and on one occasion cleared such an amazing height that she kept it to herself for fear of arousing ridicule.

Dorothy was duly selected in a team of 313 alongside nineteen other athletes, six[27] of whom had represented Great Britain in the Berlin Olympics 12 years before. Some, like Belgrave Harriers' distance runner, Bill Lucas, then aged 31, and two years Dorothy's senior, were by their own admission past their peak, but delighted to have been selected.

Sadly, several great athletes had perished in the war, while others who might have peaked in 1940 and 1944 were now past their best. One such star was diminutive British World Mile Record holder Sydney Wooderson, standing at 5' 6" tall (1.68m), and appropriately dubbed the "The Mighty Atom". He had suffered injury in the 1936 1500m, but was considered by many as the obvious candidate to carry the Olympic Torch to the cauldron in Wembley Stadium. Unfortunately, Sydney suffered the indignity of being side-lined in favour of the unknown John Mark,[28] seen by those in power as more physically suitable.

The Games Village at RAF Uxbridge, would have been something of a déjà vu for Dorothy with her war-time service still a recent memory, but like other British women athletes, she was accommodated in a hotel near Victoria Station and happily room-shared with Mitcham AC friend, Bevis Reid, a shot and discus exponent.

---

27 The 1936 and 1948 six were Norman Drake in the Hammer, Don Findlay in 110m Hurdles, Tebbs Lloyd-Johnson in 50k Walk, Laurence Reavill-Carter in Discus, Bill Roberts in 400m, and Dick Webster in the Pole Vault. In addition Whitlock competed in the walk in 1936 and again in 1952.

28 John Mark was a relatively unknown former Cambridge University student when he was controversially selected to be the final torch bearer. Many felt the honour should have gone to either Wooderson or Don Findlay, who, as well as being an Olympian, had earned a DFC during the war. John Mark was an unlucky, injury-prone sportsman, who finished 4th in the 1947 AAA Championships 440yds and represented Great Britain once over 400m against France in Paris, but who did possess "undeniable movie star good looks. "Tall and handsome like a young Greek God he stood for a moment in the sunshine, held the torch aloft to salute the concourse, then ran in perfect rhythm around the track, saluted again and lit the bowl where day and night it burned until the Games were done" . Mark went on to practise as a GP in Liss, Hampshire and died of a stroke in 1991.

ATHLETICS

at the

EMPIRE STADIUM WEMBLEY

SATURDAY AUGUST 7TH 1948

1948 London Olympics programme cover for Dorothy's day of competition.

From a field of 22, 19 women started in the high jump, the most notable absentee being Fanny Blankers-Koen who wisely decided to restrict herself to only 3 individual events, a decision justified by her success in gaining 4 gold medals.[29] All remaining competitors were still involved at the third height of 1.50m. At this point five of them incurred 3 failures and their competition was over, and another 5cm proved too much for 6 more athletes. Dorothy's team-mate Dora Gardner failed at 1.58m, along with Steinegger of Austria to finish joint 7th , and at 1.61m another 3 (Beckett of Jamaica, Britain's Bertha Crowther, and Dredge of Canada) failed to progress.

Unfortunately conscious of other events during the high jump final, our heroine was distracted on several occasions. The first came in the latter stages of the 1600m (4 x 400m) relay when Jamaican Arthur Wint dramatically pulled up having suffered a hamstring tear as he was desperately trying to close the gap on American Arthur Harnden, falling into the high jump zone. All too aware, Dorothy remembered that "...he lay there, beating the cinders in despair with the baton".

At a later stage she rushed to the trackside to cheer on South London team mate, Tom Richards, in the closing stages of the marathon soon after he lapped the track in third place. One would like to think that her shrill exhortations, added to those of the vast crowd, inspired the South London Harrier as he passed the exhausted Belgian, Étienne Gailly, and followed Argentinian victor, Delfo Cabrera, to the finish, proud winner of the silver medal[30].

Dorothy's gesture of support was a lasting memory of eyewitness teenage fan, Colin Young, who, duly inspired by these events, became an outstanding race walker, so rather incongruously remaining in touch with terra firma.

---

29 It has been suggested that the rules prevented her from doing more than 3 events, but her name did appear in the programme for the high jump.
30 Marathon result: 1st D Cabrera 2:34:31.6, 2nd T Richards 2:35:07.6 and 3rd E Gailly 2:35:33.6

With even the slowest of marathon stragglers across the safe haven of their finish, only the women's high jump remained for the crowd to watch. It was hardly surprising that most of them, including their Majesties King George VI and Queen Elizabeth stayed in their seats, all engrossed and hoping for the grand finale of an elusive British victory.

Only three athletes remained in contention when the bar reached 1.64m: Alice Coachman, the black American, who was ten times United States title winner, Micheline Ostermeyer of France already an Olympic champion[31], and the redoubtable Dorothy. At this point Dorothy would have appeared to be the favourite with no failures so far, while the other two had each accumulated 3 failures. Coachman cleared first time, Ostermeyer failed three times and Dorothy made it on her final attempt.

The sand in the landing area was thinning and the landings were clearly tough on the American's back, although it was surely similar for the enduring Dorothy. Landing correctly from using a form of the Western Roll, Coachman would most likely have landed on one leg and got further support from her hands touching down almost simultaneously. Scissors jumper Dorothy would have come down on one leg followed by the other in a quick stepping motion. One can only assume that Coachman's back problem came as she fell sideways after the initial impact.

The height was increased to 1.66m and the pair cleared it at the first attempt for a new Olympic record. At this stage Dorothy was ahead as she had had fewer failures[32]. The bar was again raised, this time to 1.68m. Coachman cleared first time, way above anything she had cleared in the States, to set another Olympic record. Dorothy followed and failed the first

---

31 As well as her bronze in the high jump Micheline Ostermeyer won gold medals in both discus and shot putt. After she retired from athletics she pursued a career as a concert pianist.
32 Sports-Reference.com shows Alice as failing once at 1.64 and 1.66, but contemporary records show that she had had 3 failures at lower heights but cleared 1.64 and 1.66 first time. The official IOC report says that up to this point Dorothy had had fewer failures.

time, but it was a case of second time lucky when she too succeeded.

Then, frustratingly, Dorothy experienced a similar scenario to the one in 1936, once again just missing the elusive gold, when the two great rivals each recorded three failures at 1.70m. Dorothy explained that she had experienced a potentially embarrassing clothing malfunction on her third attempt! "But for that bra strap mishap, the gold might have been mine!", she rued. One contemporary, who shall remain nameless disputed this, cattily suggesting that such an item of clothing was hardly necessary in Dorothy's case, although the more general opinion is that the one-time teenage Mitcham beauty queen had a figure to be envied.

As it was, the contest was over on count back, for Dorothy had taken two jumps to clear her final height to Alice's one, and the American took gold. Had Dorothy cleared the final height at the same attempt as her rival she would have been the Olympic Champion, since throughout the event she had accrued fewer failures. Ironically, had the 1936 rules applied, Dorothy would have had a good chance in a jump-off, especially as Coachman was carrying an injury.

At the conclusion of the event, Coachman, who the previous day had defied her coach and not done a workout, preferring divine intervention, "I was talking to the man above...If it is your will, it will be done", was unaware of her triumph. As The Sunday Times athletics correspondent Harold Abrahams clarified the next day,

> "Most of the crowd were unaware of the technical rules which made every jump, successful or not, a vital factor in the possible result, for if jumpers tie the fail is used to decide the issue – and Mrs Tyler was behind on failures. At 5' 5 5/8" both girls got over first time. This as it were, restored Mrs Tyler to her chance of success. Indeed when I rushed across the ground to the officials and saw the score-card it was plain that Mrs Tyler could win it if both

failed completely at the next height for an Olympic record[33].

Again, Miss Coachman got over at her first jump. Mrs Tyler failed. Although the crowd didn't know it yet, that really was the end. Dorothy probably did know, but she was not disheartened and at her second attempt the roar of the crowd showed that she had got over"

"Alice wasn't sure what would happen next. There were no ties in the Olympics. Then she saw her name on the board...

.. "1st COACHMAN, UNITED STATES"
Unlucky Dorothy had to settle for silver, albeit a splendidly earned one, once more".

She did, however, have the consolation of jointly holding the new Olympic record.

With hindsight, Dorothy was surprisingly more philosophical. Not so long ago she said,

"Coming second was not as important as it is today. You were thrilled to do what you did. You didn't get the coverage you do today, where it's only to do with money. We weren't celebrities because there was no television where now you are on every week. I think it was more fun then. We were all friends and I don't think they all are now. I don't think I would like to be taking part now".

In the Official Report of The Organising Committee for the XIV Olympiad, it was recorded that
"The high jump produced one of the most thrilling duels imaginable", but there was no mention of the distractions!

---

33 When Dorothy had two failures at 1.64, this meant Alice was ahead if they both failed
1.66. When both cleared 1.66 first time, Dorothy was now ahead. In the event of a tie, the
winner is decided on who took fewer attempts at the final height. If both clear the final
height at the same attempt, the total number of failures would decide the winner.

Sadly the search for an action shot of Dorothy during the competition proved to be fruitless, but it led to a fascinating conversation with Muriel Hearnshaw (née Pletts) who, as a 17-year- old sprinter found herself, like Dorothy 12 years earlier, the baby of the team. While Dorothy had had the benefit of several friends in the team, Muriel as the sole Northerner was more isolated. It sounds as though the team management did little to put this right.

Her father, who had by then left the family, did at least recognise his daughter's achievement by sending her a letter of congratulation. Dorothy, for her part, conceded that without the massive support of husband Dick and her mother, who looked after the boys on the run up to the games, she would certainly not have been so successful.

The competition against Coachman, however, made Dorothy go 100% for the Western Roll technique which she had been experimenting with since before the war, but could not get above the magic 5 foot barrier. The acquisition of a coach became imperative and successful contact was then made with Arthur Gold leading to long overdue progress.

Later in the year, Dorothy cleared 1.65m for a notable individual win in the France v England encounter at the Colombes Stadium, although the hosts went on to win the team match.

1949 saw Dorothy touring Italy as the star of the Surrey County team, and she duly won all three high jump competitions. Her first match clearance of 1.65m in Reine proved to be far and away her best.

In the women's All Time List published in 1950 from Soviet comparative scoring tables, Dorothy ranked 13th in the world and 2nd in Britain for the high jump since records began.

That same year she was honoured with the England women's team captaincy for the Empire Games in Auckland, New

Zealand. Most farewells were made at London's Waterloo station on 16th December prior to departure on the 11.38am boat train to Southampton. The athletes had assembled as instructed, with two suitcases, one clearly marked "Wanted on the voyage", and the other ready to be consigned to a hold, where there would only be access at agreed times each week. They were also checked as being in possession of their passports, international vaccination certificates, plus their ration books, lingering signs of post-war privation.

One reporter wrote "Centre of a big contingent was Mrs Dorothy Tyler, who in turn picked up David and Barry, her two small sons, who seemed bewildered by the bustle and clung tightly to their Christmas toys. Dorothy wore a good luck floral horse-shoe, a gift from Mitcham AC. The boys were far from happy to see their mother departing for the far side of the world just before Christmas".

It was further decreed in their instructions that the whole team would dine in the B deck saloon on special tables "Set aside for the purpose...there is no need to sit in the same seat for each meal ...it will be all to the good if seats were changed". Suitably informed, Dorothy sailed on this, her second such voyage to the southern hemisphere with most of the England team. Forty-one team members went aboard the S.S.Tamaroa on 16th December at Southampton, scheduled to arrive in New Zealand on 21st January, two weeks before the opening ceremony. These privileged athletes were the last Britons to travel to a major international competition by ship to the other side of the world.

The Tamaroa, which at 12,405 tons was modest in comparison to huge stabilised modern cruise liners, gave the athletes a "wild water ride" as she battled her way out of the Channel and into the potentially more testing waters of the Bay of Biscay. Reuters reported that the girl athletes stood up to the stormy weather well, as did the swimmers, but on the other hand the cyclists and the wrestlers were not so resilient, and had "all been down because of the bad weather. Many had been forced to retire to their cabins".

Despite her size, the Tamaroa presented something of a bonus to these ambitious athletes en route to New Zealand. She boasted a recreation area, and a fine promenade deck which was reserved twice a day for runners to train, albeit on a "tight track", but otherwise unimpeded. Deck games were also provided and dances laid on, which enabled the athletes to socialise and relax on the long voyage across the Atlantic Ocean. On board entertainment included a sumptuous Christmas dinner featuring so many choices as to be thoroughly confusing, an official Shaw Savill Line Horse Race Meeting in which Dorothy owned "Mr Higgins by Team out of bed". Five days before they arrived in New Zealand, a Grand Sea Revue appropriately entitled "Completely at Sea", and featuring Sylvia Cheeseman among the cast, was staged for the entertainment of all on board. It was noted in the programme that "Any connection between the characters and anything human is purely miraculous". A luxurious farewell dinner rounded off what must have been a floating experience of a lifetime.

On the first stop at Curacao in the Dutch West Indies on 28th December, a "well equipped stadium" was made available for their use, though there was no mention of a track. The only stadium existing in Willemstad at the time was the Rif Stadium, which could only have boasted a grass track on its reportedly stony surface. Research has failed to reveal whether the athletes availed themselves of the questionable opportunity! Then it was full steam ahead for Balbao, and the fascinating negotiation of the six locks of The Panama Canal, which involved a 26m rise and descent, and onwards into the Pacific Ocean, heading for Auckland where their 37-day voyage finished on 31st January 1950.

It was during the final on-board dance before arrival that the athletics team manager Mrs Taylor was in disagreement with the overall England team Commandant, Mr J. W. Taylor, over women athletes' curfew times. Dorothy dutifully returned to her shared cabin together with Margaret Walker in accordance with the edict of her manager. Meanwhile, the few females who remained on the dance floor were predictably much in demand. Jean Desforges (later Pickering) was the last to be caught as the male revellers passed her adroitly one to another, away from the increasingly irate Mrs Taylor.

When the other occupants of the cabin eventually got back, they found to their consternation, the door locked and Dorothy unresponsive. Short term "safe haven" was found with friendly swimmers and divers who were not under such strict regimentation. Dorothy eventually reported her colleagues' absence, which was very much down to her action and lack of response and there was a great deal of ill feeling. Were Dorothy's actions an attempt to protect herself after the events in Australia 12 years earlier? – whatever it was, her attitude seems ironic. I tried to get more detail out of diver Edna Child, but even after all this time she declined to sneak on her friends.

The rest of the team flew out over a month later with little chance of controversy, on board a BOAC Constellation airliner, which took a mere five days to complete the journey! Their flight routed via Rome, Cairo, Karachi, Calcutta, Singapore, Batavia[34], Darwin and Sydney, before eventually landing at Auckland in New Zealand on 21st January.

Athletes were advised of postal arrangements which meant that a ½ ounce letter home taking seven or eight days, would cost 1 shilling and 3 pence, with the same for each additional ½ ounce. Airmail letters were available at the post offices, price 6 pence.

On Tuesday February 7th at the grass track in Eden Park, Auckland, Dorothy triumphed in the high jump as England's only female athlete to take gold, matching her Berlin silver medal height of 5' 3" (1.60m). She won on fewest failures

---

34 *Modern-day Jakarta. The name changed just before they flew to Auckland, when Indonesia became independent.*

ahead of team-mate Bertha Crowther (Middlesex Ladies AC), while New Zealander Noeline Swanton took a distant third with 5' 1" (1.55m). This time the count back rule was in her favour. Showing her versatility, Dorothy also threw the javelin 107' 9 ¼" (32.85m) for fourth place, again ahead of Crowther, and finished a respectable 8th in long jump too. The men did better, winning five gold medals, but their best effort in the high jump was only fifth place.

After the Games, the athletes had further competition at Lancaster Park, where Dorothy won her speciality at 5' 0" ahead of Canadian Elaine Silburn. The athletes later travelled to Timaru, South Canterbury for a multi-sports extravaganza at The Caledonian Grounds. There she took part in a handicap high jump challenge from which no results seem to have survived. Dorothy and her colleagues felt like "celebs" when they performed in front of more large and enthusiastic crowds.

During this trip down under, a seemingly harmless prank, the nature of which has not until now been publicly revealed, escalated enough for two sprinters (believed to be Doris Batter and Sylvia Cheeseman) to be called to account at the Women's Amateur Athletics Association headquarters once back in London. The conspirators had achieved an effect way beyond their wildest dreams. Their "crime" was to make a very effective apple-pie bed[35] for their humourless team manager. This provoked wrath in the extreme, instead of a sporting smile, with their behaviour being condemned as "not amenable to discipline". As team captain, Dorothy was also called to account, but the measure of her involvement, if any, in the prank has never been fully revealed.

Dorothy was later reported in the press as saying "It is a lot of fuss about nothing. I have been taking part in international sports for 15 years; I am a judge and have done more coaching for the WAAA than anyone else; I have done all I can for

---

35 The bottom sheet is folded over and made to look like the top sheet. When the victim gets into bed their feet cannot get more than half-way down the bed.

women's athletics and I feel I should be above reproach".

She did not attend the enquiry, opting for a coaching commitment at Bedford Physical Training College. It was a regular arrangement, and her explanation to the committee was accepted. Dorothy later visited the WAAA Secretary, Mrs Hughes, who assured her that the matter was closed. The sprinters were excluded from the European Championships, but that was the end of the matter.

Captain or culprit, Dorothy's popularity with the powers that be clearly fluctuated, but she was certainly not one to be ignored!

In a separate issue, a female athlete had merited disapproval by showing too keen an interest in a colleague of the opposite sex. In due course, they subsequently married and "lived happily ever after". Despite all this, it was reported that "The behaviour of the English team throughout was excellent. They were most popular wherever they went and upheld the reputation of their country on all occasions".

Home again, Dorothy went back to work as a part-time secretary, mother and housewife. Young Barry Tyler celebrated his mother's return with a display of sandcastle flags, questioning Dick, "Daddy, is this mummy?" In her absence, Barry and older brother David had taken it in turns to share their parents' bed with their father.

In the 1950 European Championships held in the Heysel Stadium Brussels, on an atrocious take off, Dorothy was one of three women to clear 1.63m. As in Wembley, she finished second on count back, this time to Sheila Alexander, with Galina Ganeker of the USSR third. Once again, luck was not on her side and the count-back rule had frustratingly tipped the balance.

Now Dorothy's supremacy of British women's high jumping was being given a truly significant challenge from tall athlete and international netballer, Sheila Alexander, who was one of the new breed of straddle jumpers. The straddle was slightly superior to the Western Roll, but both gave a great advantage over the scissors jump that Dorothy had used, since the body didn't have to go so far above the bar.[36]

The time was clearly right to abandon the faithful old scissors jump technique. Dorothy finally decided to "grasp the nettle" and at last really go for the Western Roll. So in 1951, still determined to progress and with the "Western" mastered, she ambitiously abandoned her dated "scissors" after twenty years in competition and committed to the new technique. Highly respected "NUT"[37] Andrew Huxtable said a few years later "One can only speculate on the heights she might have achieved earlier with this style and also had the war not interrupted her career". Without this major change her international career would have almost certainly ground to a halt. With the help of top coach Arthur Gold, she rejuvenated her high jump career, learning the more sophisticated and efficient Western Roll technique.

Acutely aware of Dorothy's unwavering quest for Olympic gold, the great Harold Abrahams, and writer of repute, possibly in the hope of inspiring our heroine, presented her with a copy of a book entitled "With the Skin of their Teeth, Great Sporting Finishes"[38]. He wrote inside

"To Dorothy Tyler with every good wish that the third time may be lucky,
Harold M Abrahams
December 1951"

Abrahams perhaps more out of loyalty than conviction, may have still felt that Dorothy had the potential to take the

---

36 *See Appendix C*
37 *Member of the National Union of Track Statisticians*
38 *Full title "With the skin of their teeth: Memories of great sporting finishes in golf, cricket, rugby and association football, lawn tennis, boxing, athletics, rowing and horse-racing". It was written by Guy "Gully" Nickalls, a member of a great rowing dynasty and like Dorothy twice an Olympic silver medallist.*

Olympic title, hoping maybe that he could help motivate her towards it.

Significantly, within the contents was a chapter entitled

"A BRILLIANT WOMAN HIGH JUMPER"

which stated ..
"Great Britain has yet to win a women's event in athletics at the Olympic Games and one of the most gallant and most unlucky performers has been Dorothy Tyler. Twice she came within an ace of victory in the Olympic high jump – twice she failed, if failure can really describe what happened".

But the clouds of challenge had clearly been gathering; for Dorothy's teenage world record mark of 1.66m in 1939 had been equalled twice during 1941, first by Esther Van Helden (RSA) at Stellenbosch, and then by Swiss jumper, Ilsebill Pfenning, and eclipsed two years later by Fanny Blankers-Koen, the fast emerging flying Dutchwoman who broke the 1.70m barrier by a centimetre in Amsterdam for a clear World Record. More significantly, how could Abrahams not have recognised the immediate domestic challenge of the 1950 and 1951 Women's AAA defeats inflicted on Dorothy by Sheila Alexander-Lerwill, whose wonderful winning 1.72m clearance in the latter championship established another World Record for Britain? Sheila not only had the advantage of youth and height; she was employing the increasingly popular and technically more efficient straddle technique.

With her younger rival very much in the ascendancy, the long-time Mitcham scissors jumper had only been able to move one technical step forward, albeit a major one for her as she started to compete successfully using the Western Roll. Coach, Arthur Gold, was fulsome in his praise for Dorothy, by then well into the autumn of her career, as she could so easily have avoided the challenge and retired gracefully.

No easy task, the change of technique was the more so for one well into the autumn of her career. This must have demanded courage as well as dedication to the task in hand. To take off from her favoured right foot, Dorothy had to relearn her approach, now having to attack the bar from the right. Instead of rapidly swinging her inside left leg, the "Western" called for a very different, rapid drive up of a now bending right leg. The bar clearance was changed from a much modified "seated" position to a right hip down "on the side" position. The landing moved on from a left-right foot succession in the sand to a "tripod touch down" on to both hands and the right leg.

She could have been forgiven had she not grasped the nettle and taken the easy, as seen by some, option of avoiding the challenge, gracefully retiring then and resting on her most worthily gained laurels, but Dorothy proved once more that she was made of sterner stuff.

Also emerging in the wings at this time was a talented Anglo/Irish teenager, Thelma Hopkins, who competed against Dorothy for the first time in 1951, and who she remembers as a sporting and helpful star, ready to pass on tips concerning the Western Roll technique. Little could they then have realised that in the 15-year-old Thelma, there was another world record holder and Olympic high jump silver medallist starting out on such a similar path to Dorothy's.

She was one of eleven women worldwide, headed by Lerwill, who had cleared 1.60m or more in 1951, with Soviet Aleksandra Chudina, South African Esta Brand and Feodora Schenk (formerly zu Solms) now representing Austria. Considered opinion at the time was that, for various reasons, challenge to the Britons in 1952 would come from another quarter, the petite Soviet stylist, Galina Ganeker who had earlier tied with Lerwill and beaten Tyler.

Having relinquished her hold on the UK high jump record, Dorothy set another, when she very successfully put her versatility to the competitive test in only the third WAAA Pentathlon Championship in 1951 held at the Snaresbrook Park

Track, Ilford. She won with a British record 3224 points[39] with performances of 220yds 27.5sec, 80m hurdles 12.1sec, high jump 5ft 4in, long jump 17ft 9in, and shot 25ft 5½ins. On that day, Dorothy was in a class of her own, beating the runner-up and previous title holder, Bertha Crowther, by the clear margin of 76 points.

---

39 *This was changed to 3953 points with the introduction of new scoring tables. Until 1954 different countries had their own scoring tables. As the events used also changed over the years, direct comparisons are very difficult.*

Chapter 4
TWICE MORE AN OLYMPIAN..

Dorothy, by then a mother of two, had relinquished her UK number one spot to Lerwill, but was duly selected on merit for her third Olympic appearance at the 1952 Games in Helsinki. The occasion was notable for the post-war re-appearance of the Soviet Union for the first time in 40 years, and their Eastern Bloc allies were there in force too.

With rationing still in place, perks for the privileged Olympians had been almost as welcome as in 1948, and alongside nutritious dairy products, a coveted supply of sweets, for many, topped such governmental generosity.

By July 1st, Dorothy was well on her way towards Helsinki selection, second equal in the world high jump rankings behind the Soviet Chudina's 1.66m, and alongside Lerwill at 1.65m.

The British team assembled in London on 15th July at the Eccleston Hotel at 0800 hours B.S.T and later travelled by coach to Bovingdon Airport for the departure of their flight to Helsinki. It was noted in the British Olympic Association Games handbook, that "Hats for the men's team will be fitted at the Eccleston Hotel before departure and all are asked to be punctual". Bovingdon Airport, then an R.A.F. facility and now featuring a prison among other things, accommodated the four-engined Avro York aircraft specially emblazoned with the Olympic rings, which flew the aspiring athletes across the North Sea to Finland.

At 90 plus, anyone can be forgiven for having misty memories, and one such recall of Dorothy's led me down a fascinating diversion. "We had a surprising welcome when nearing Helsinki; we were met by two big fighter planes". Following up on Dorothy's somewhat intriguing but vague story, it became apparent that an incident had occurred but not involving her flight.

Sprinter and later journalist, Sylvia Cheeseman, was sure that it was a different flight, and most likely to have been the one carrying Great Britain team manager, Jack Crump, and not theirs. More specifically too, she confirmed that MIG, rather than "Big" fighters, had been involved.

Fellow high jumper and later world record holder, Sheila Lerwill, confirmed a strong "niggle" at the back of her mind about an incident, but could not recall anything more specific than confirming that nothing untoward happened and that their flight, as far as she was aware, was not involved in any mid-air incident.

Closer research involving one of the Skyways flight cabin crew confirmed, without any great detail, that an incident, requiring investigation and an overnight stay in the YMCA, did take place. This gentleman certainly flew a jumper to the Olympics, but not an athlete. His special passenger turned out to be Britain's sole gold medallist, the legendary horse, Foxhunter, which Col. Harry Llewellyn rode to victory.

Jack Crump, the Great Britain men's team manager provided the clearest evidence of what actually happened, in his book "Running Round the World".

"We noticed fighter aircraft swooping around us.[40] We took this to be a kind of welcoming escort from our Finnish hosts.....later I met the British Air attaché in Helsinki.....he expressed the view that we were lucky....we had been buzzed by Soviet fighters for an alleged incursion into their territory and it was only the fact that our markings showed us to be an Olympic

---

40 It seems most likely that the Skyways York flight had strayed into nearby Soviet air space, above some former Finnish territory on the Porkkala Peninsula and the neighbouring one of Uppiniemi. Both had been ceded to the Soviet Union as war reparations in 1944, and supported naval and air bases. It could have been that the British team flight had come too near for the Soviets' comfort. It might then have been picked up on their local radar, which would have led to the scrambling of the battle flight to intercept and most fortunately to redirect them.

team that we had been permitted to continue our flight!"

One would like to think that the Soviet air force pilots, with their country back in the fold for the Helsinki games, and recognising the five symbolic rings on either side of the fuselage, acted with compassion.

Further referring to Soviet insularity Dorothy said,

> "They insisted on having their own separate village and training facilities, while all the other men's teams occupied the main village and the women were housed in a college. The Eastern Bloc athletes were very wary of being seen fraternising with the rest of us. But this came to nothing when it poured with rain while we were waiting for the parade, and we ended up sheltering in the ladies' toilet with a group of large Russian men....all barriers were broken!"

The Soviets and other Eastern Bloc teams had their own "Village" in University of Technology at Otaniemi 20 minutes away from the main accommodation, and nearer their sensitive military bases on territory ceded by the Finns to the Soviets as part of war reparations.

Much had improved for the athletes since 1948, and the younger Bill Nankeville, then in his second Olympics, has appreciative memories of the 24-hour canteen and its vast range of international fare. Sadly for him, although impressive and readily available, the food was no cure for flu which struck him on the still straw-strewn aircraft which had earlier carried the golden horse.

Dorothy recounted that the biggest roar from crowd was generated by former Finnish athletics hero, Paavo Nurmi, happily reintegrated after a sad sortie into professionalism, as he strode proudly around his home stadium carrying the Olympic Flame. He was once again firmly established as a national icon.

The women's high jump in Helsinki attracted the smallest field of any event, seventeen, with Dorothy still sharing the Olympic record at 1.68m, the sole survivor from the 1936 Games. It was also remarkable that no one else in the event had competed in the London Olympics four years earlier.

Tyler's reluctant and consequently uncomfortable room-mate there was Sheila Lerwill, the new British World record holder. Lerwill caused a ripple of concern when registering a miss at 1.50m. Seven athletes remained in contention at 1.61m but Dorothy, strapped because of an untimely stomach muscle strain, was one of the unfortunate five who failed. She eventually had to settle for a commendable equal 7th with a 1.58m clearance. It is worth noting that historically then only thirty women had cleared the next height to be tackled. Now it was Sheila Lerwill's turn, tired and bleeding from a spike injury, to take a frustrating third successive Olympic high jump silver for Britain, with a clearance of 1.65m. Yorkshire born Thelma Hopkins from Northern Ireland, following in the Odam mould as a 16-year-old Olympic debutante, finished a fine fourth at 1.58m, the same as Dorothy but with fewer failures.

Here in Helsinki, the ungainly but all conquering Czech, Emil Zatopek, inevitably caught her eye together with those of many thousands more enthralled spectators, as he ate up the miles, accumulating an astonishing triple golden tally in the 5000m, 10,000m and marathon. Also noted was a young Roger Bannister who finished 4th in the 1500m behind the relatively unknown Josy Barthel of Luxembourg.

According to Dorothy, the Helsinki Olympics were considered to have been conducted more closely to the Olympic ideal of founder Baron Pierre de Coubertin than any others.

That October, the Great Britain women's team suffered a surprise defeat at the hands of the Italians in Naples, but Dorothy, the high jump winner at 1.65m salvaged some satisfaction and national pride by being credited with the award for the meeting's best performance.

XV OLYMPIA HELSINKI 1952

YLEISURHEILU

ATHLETISME · ATHLETICS · FRI-IDROTT

OLYMPIASTADION
HELSINKI · HELSINGFORS

SUNNUNTAI DIMANCHE
SUNDAY SÖNDAG

27. 7.

PÄIVÄOHJELMA PROGRAMME JOURNALIER
DAILY PROGRAMME DAGSPROGRAM

100 mk

1952 Helsinki Olympics programme cover for Dorothy's day of competition

Despite now being in her thirties, Dorothy decided to continue competing. She owed much to devoted husband Dick and her mother who shouldered a great deal of the maternal role which, of necessity, she sacrificed in pursuit of further athletic goals. Such was Dorothy's consistency in the 1950s, that her high jump success in the London v Moscow (virtually a USSR team!) was blandly recorded alongside Jean Desforges' (Pickering) long jump victory as "...their usual success".

Empire & Commonwealth Games' captaincy was again bestowed on her for the England women's team in Vancouver in 1954, where she won the high jump silver medal and was placed a very creditable 5th in the javelin. Thelma Hopkins of Northern Ireland was a comfortable winner at 5' 6" (1.67m) ahead of the redoubtable Dorothy and Alice Whitty of Canada, who both cleared 5' 3" (1.60m) for silver and bronze medals respectively. Sheila Lerwill was 4th with 5' 2" (1.57m), and she soon retired to concentrate on her first love sport of netball.

After the high jump the competitors were much in demand from the press photographers and Canadian bronze medallist Alice Whitty recalled that while both she and winner Thelma Hopkins were immediately happy to face the cameras, Dorothy with her own agenda, was not. She insisted on getting out her make-up bag. She then applied lipstick, and made sure that her blonde hair was neatly brushed. Only when the final touch of a silk Olympic scarf had been neatly tied in place did Dorothy join the others for the photo-call.

Barry and David's concern over their mother's absence in Canada was eased on her return, following excited cries of

"What have you got for us?"

Two Mountie uniforms, unheard of in England at the time, were revealed. The boys' slight disappointment at the absence of hats soon faded as they were able to integrate plastic revolvers and "Bullets" into their battles from behind the sofa. So much for present day health and safety restrictions!

Dorothy was unable to explain that she achieved two other international wins and a second later in the same year.

From then on, sons Barry and David became much more involved with their mother's athletics training, at first playing in the sandpits, and attending competitions. It was not long though before mother had eased them into some basic training routines. They got a buzz from the attentions of the press, many of the photographs still featuring somewhat dog-eared in the family collection. Dorothy, too, enjoyed the limelight with her blonde hair and trim figure, dress sense self-evident. Important venues like Buckingham Palace and The Hilton were still very much part of the Tylers' life.

Early in 1955, the "Whip and Carrot" magazine of the specialist high jump jumpers' club featured Dorothy in one of its leading articles, in which she was described as the world's greatest woman athlete by its unidentified author, who wrote,

> "Obviously when writing of the world's greatest, one should not treat it lightly. Far too often we hear of so-called experts talking glibly *of The world's greatest, genius* and other similar phrases used – in the main - without thought or discretion.
>
> Why then am I doing likewise? The answer is simple. I am not doing likewise.
> And why not, you may ask? Again the answer is simple. I am not writing without thought or discretion. Many years of thought and experience are behind this article, and I can assure my readers that I have used the above heading only after long and careful consideration. I am convinced that after studying this short article, most knowledgeable followers of athletics will agree with me".

Apparently, Dorothy, on receiving a request to fill in gaps in his text, replied by return, despite suffering a "very bad dose of flu" (as were Dick and her mother too) plus concern over son

David, who had just been brought home covered in blood after an encounter with a lamp post - he had been taken to hospital to have his head stitched.

Dorothy recorded her final international victory for Great Britain against France in one of five international appearances in 1955, with a relatively modest height of 1.59m ahead of Audrey Bennett, to complete an amazing 18-year span of international successes. At the end of the season, Thelma Hopkins headed the world rankings with a best of 1.71m, while the ever game Tyler ranked equal 6th alongside Aleksandra Chudina on 1.66m.

She represented her country in three more international matches during the Olympic year 1956 and the Melbourne Games were still in the ever-competitive Tyler's sights, but she was, in the event, in debt to lady luck for selection. Still jumping well, but not really in contention for honours, she was on hand when a rival for selection succumbed to injury, and she was picked to represent Great Britain for her fourth Olympics.

Having won her first Women's AAA title in 1936 at the age of sixteen, she rounded off the series twenty years later in 1956 with her victory over an emerging sixteen-year-old talent, Mary Bignal, who went on to win Olympic long jump gold in 1964. By that time Dorothy had amassed eight titles and been runner up four times. She eyed the prospect hopefully, but with the realism of one in the twilight of her career. Subject to selection the 36-year-old said, "If I go it will not be as favourite, but win or lose, it would be nice to return to Australia where I won my first Empire title in 1938".

In a pre-Olympic magazine interview with Sub-4-minute-mile pioneer Roger Bannister, who was heading for Melbourne not as a competitor but as a commentator, Dorothy was as forthright as ever when asked about being unfortunate not to win a medal in the pre-war Berlin Games

"In 1936 the rules were that in case of a tie, you went on jumping until one of you either failed or got over it, so that although I tied for first place, I was beaten in a jump off".

Bannister then asked,

"And is it true that if the rule remained as it was in 1936 you would have won your gold medal in 1948?"
"After the 1936 Games they were a little tired of us having to jump off. It took so long that they altered the rules. These rules applied in 1948, and I tied again for first place, as you know and the old rules would have given me the gold medal".[41]

Just once more the Tyler family rallied round to look after the boys to enable their mother to travel to Australia. Inconvenient in the extreme for the British athletes, the 1956 Olympics being held in Australia were way out of season and involved one of the longest and most arduous journeys imaginable. Dorothy's group allocated to Qantas flight EM514/236A was in the charge of Jack Crump, a top British official, and the itinerary featured stops at Cairo, and Karachi with a night stop-over in Singapore with accommodation at the Raffles or Ocean Park Hotel.

In the event, with international incidents, the Hungarian uprising and the Suez Crisis looming large, the flight was 24 hours late departing. A late evening departure aboard the Lockheed Constellation prompted the team management to separate the men and women, with the latter occupying the front of the plane "so that if anyone wanted to remove clothing for the night flight this could be done without embarrassment. We had a little difficulty in securing compliance with this firm decision, but the team co-operated splendidly all the way to Melbourne".

---

41 *In Dorothy's opinion, she felt that Alice Coachman would not have been able to contest a jump off as in 1936, due to her deteriorating back condition.*

ATHLETICS

MAIN STADIUM
(Melbourne Cricket Ground)

SATURDAY, 1ST DECEMBER, 1956

OFFICIAL PROGRAMME - ONE SHILLING

1956 Melbourne Olympics programme cover for Dorothy's day of competition

Athens became the first stop where most enjoyed "a good bacon and egg breakfast". But then the politically charged Greeks placed pamphlets about alleged RAF atrocities around the airport lounge, and like a red flag to a bull this provoked serving airman Derek Ibbotson to tear one up and throw it in a bin.

Only Crump's calm application of experience with the threat of the British Ambassador and prompt work of the aircrew ensured a timely departure on the next leg of the journey.

The overnight stop at Singapore did reveal one ripple of defiance when two male athletes broke the curfew and had to be removed from a well-known night spot. Their absence had been discovered when the team management went on a room tour to issue anti-malaria tablets!

In due course the Mitcham AC athlete, by then 36 years of age, made her fourth and final Olympic Games appearance, in Melbourne. Again, the determined Dorothy reached the high jump final. She competed with her traditional flair, clearing the very respectable height of 1.60m to share 12th place. Colleague Thelma Hopkins, sixteen years her junior, succeeded at 1.67m for a shared silver medal place. This was the fourth successive time that a Briton had won a silver medal in the women's high jump, and the sequence continued when Dorothy Shirley again won silver at the 1960 Olympics.

Dorothy's 20-year Olympic high jump marathon had finally run its course in Melbourne when she dislodged the bar for the third time at 1.64m, and both she and the bar landed unceremoniously together in the sand. Her 12th place was no disgrace for an athlete aged 36, and ahead of Britain's other competitor Audrey Bennett who finished 16th.

As she bowed gracefully out of the "Big Time" down under, her lasting memory is perhaps understandably not of her own event, but of the men's steeplechase, and the drama which emanated from it. Britain's third choice, Chris Brasher, had joyfully crossed the line first, only to be disqualified for allegedly impeding a rival. It is reported that Brasher's subsequent reinstatement was in no small measure thanks to the sportsmanship of his alleged victim who said that the incident made no difference to the result.

This time, their mother's absence for the boys had been shortened by air travel, and eased by television. Further soothing was clearly derived courtesy of some of the Games' sponsors who had provided 144 bottles of Lucozade, plus a generous supply of Horlicks and Ovaltine.

Later, presents of books revealing strange creatures like the Duck-billed Platypus, and other souvenirs from "Down Under", the most prized of which were a pair of authentic "come-back" aboriginal boomerangs, rekindled the youngsters' good cheer. These provided prestigious fun, but did at times cause close calls, most notably when one broke in the road having narrowly missed a car!

An interesting story came to light after Dorothy's death. Derek Pritchard, a former teacher at Gorringe Park School, recalled that Dorothy had not forgotten her roots. He reported that she sent a supply of cooking fat for every pupil and member of staff at the school.

When she retired from international athletics in 1956, Dorothy was still reigning British high jump champion. She had competed in 38 internationals, won 14 National titles, 12 in the high jump. Such was her club spirit and appetite for the sport that she continued competing for her beloved Mitcham AC for many more years and so successful was she that she set 14 world "Age" bests from 33 to 46 years of age, with many an aspiring young athlete having to concede to her in competition. Dorothy retired from "serious" high jumping in 1959, but continued at a low-key level until 1966 when she decided to stick to terra firma. Even then, she maintained her fitness as she showed when, at the age of 50, she ran a lap as part of the Mitcham AC Golden Jubilee celebrations. Her rock-solid consistency is obvious from the graph plotting her annual best performances from 1934 to 1963 in Appendix D.

At the end of 1956 she still featured prominently in the world lists at 15th equal, alongside two Soviet athletes Sofiya Garms and Yelena Kudrayavtseva, Austrian Reineide Knapp, Australian Carol Bernoth and fellow Briton Audrey Bennett, all having cleared 1.65m. The following year she set a world V35 best of 5' 6" (1.68m) matching her personal best from way back in 1948. This was achieved using built-up shoes that were subsequently banned.

Early on during the build-up to the 1958 Empire and Commonwealth Games in Cardiff, Dorothy's younger friend and former rival, Canadian Alice Whitty, who was curiously omitted from her national team, had travelled independently to Britain to watch the Games. When they met up and she explained the situation to Dorothy, our heroine was appalled at Alice's omission, and thinking quickly, asked, "Where were you born?" "Canada", came the clear response adding quickly, "but hang on a minute, father was born in England!" "Well then leave it to me", said Dorothy, who promptly set about investigating whether this was a real possibility.

She soon returned to ask, "Would you consider jumping for us?"

While appreciating the initiative, Alice, established as a patriotic Canadian, graciously declined and enjoyed the Games as a spectator. On return to Vancouver her disappointed father said that she had made a mistake, but she believed that she made the right decision and stands by it to this day.

Illustrations 1957 - 2012

Examples of Dorothy's artwork

Dorothy dancing with Michael Somes to learn ballet as a training aid

Dorothy putting ballet into practice with her training group (5th from left is Olympian Gwenda Matthews)

Dorothy hurdling with her son Barry

Dorothy, far right, officiating at White City while Yolanda
Balas clears, 1962

Eagle-eyed Dorothy, left, helping to check the winning height

Mitcham AC visit to Rotterdam 1965. Dorothy centre and the great Fanny Blankers-Koen 2nd left

Dick Fosbury wins gold at the 1968 Mexico Olympics and changes high-jumping forever (Mark Shearman photo)

Dorothy as Team Manager in Bruges 1969, with Maureen
Tranter, Madeleine Weston and Barbara Inkpen

D. Tye

CROHAM HURST GOLF CLUB

Handicap 18 · L.G.U. 72

Marker's Score	Hole	Yards	Par	Stroke	Score	Result	Marker's Score	Hole	Yards	Par	Stroke	Score	Result
	1	401	5	10	7		6	10	390	4	3	6	
	2	383	4	2	7	·	4	11	164	3	15	①	
	3	256	4	13	5			12	396	5	5	7	
	4	257	4	8	5			13	163	3	17	4	
	5	158	3	18	4			14	364	4	7	4	
	6	479	5	4	7			15	452	5	1	5	
	7	125	3	16	4			16	198	3	14	5	
	8	468	5	6	5			17	290	4	9	4	
	9	367	4	12	7			18	393	4	11	6	
OUT ...		2894	37		51		IN ...		2810	35		42	42
							OUT ...		2894	37		51	51
							TOTAL		5704	72		93	93

Marker's Signature ... D T Tyes

Player's Signature ... M Gorner

Date 14/4/70

HANDICAP ... 18 18

NET SCORE ... 75 75

Her hole in one golf card, 1970

Dorothy receives her MBE from the Prince of Wales

The Tyler family at the Palace. L to R Barry, Dick, Dorothy, and David

Dorothy still demonstrating a good golf swing, aged 82
(Mark Shearman photo)

QUEEN
OF THE
TRACK

ALICE COACHMAN
OLYMPIC HIGH-JUMP CHAMPION

For Dorothy
You inspire us all to keep
dreaming BIG and jumping high!
Best wishes,
Heather Lang

Alice Coachman

HEATHER LANG
ILLUSTRATED BY FLOYD COOPER

BOYDS MILLS PRESS
HONESDALE, PENNSYLVANIA

Alice Coachman's book with a dedication to Dorothy

Dorothy, Official Starter of the 2012 London Marathon.
(Roger Miller photo)

Dorothy being interviewed on TV by Sue Barker

Gaby Bailey

Kate Ferguson

Keya Patel

The winning replacement cover designs by girls from Old Palace School, Croydon year 5

Dorothy with her two Olympic silver medals and 1936 torch

Reunion of old Olympians in 2012.
L to R Ron Cooper, Edna Child, Dorothy, Sylvia Disley, John Disley

Chapter 5
THE PAY-BACK YEARS

With all her achievements, expertise and experience, Dorothy was naturally drawn to putting something back into the sport which she so dearly loved. Her stated ambition in 1957 was "To be a first class official and coach", and so began the 40 fruitful years which she primarily devoted to coaching. The coaching career dovetailed smoothly into her gradually reducing competitive programme for a further ten years during which she continued to jump and throw enthusiastically at club level for her beloved Mitcham A.C.

Dorothy made the most of her WRAF Physical Training Qualification and sporting versatility when she started teaching at the Links School in Mitcham. The AAA star Award Scheme of the 1970s was right up her street, and through her enthusiasm employed to good effect, many of her young charges exceeded their own expectations of achievement. Later, she moved on to work at the Rowan School in Mitcham, sharing classroom duties with sport. Former pupil Lorna Boothe recalls,
> "I was lucky as a youngster as Dorothy was one of my favourite PE teachers at Rowan High School for Girls as well as club coach at Mitcham AC. I was a very energetic youngster and bit of a rascal as she reminded me when we met up just before London 2012. I remember with fond memories at the age of 12 I won the school cross country and Dorothy presented me one of her own medals, which I have to this day. When she gave it to me she said, "I hope you will get many more".

What better inspiration can a youngster have?

Dorothy's input must have helped Lorna's athletic career en route to her becoming a double Olympian, Commonwealth Games gold medallist, and later a highly respected coach and international team manager.

In 1959, she was voted Britain's greatest ever woman athlete by the massively well-informed National Union of Track Statisticians. In the same year, when honoured with the Presidency of Mitcham AC, she cleared 5' 3" (1.60m) in her specialist event, the same height over which she had so significantly sailed in 1935! Dorothy took to coaching like a duck to water and soon successfully established herself in that role as an innovative enthusiast. Together with club colleague Kath Dale she became joint first female qualifier for the Amateur Athletic Association Honorary Coach award in August 1960. Four years later she became an Honorary Senior Coach.

By then honoured with the Presidency of the Surrey County Women's A.A.A, which she had served so well, she spoke of her pride at the annual Mitcham AC Dinner while shielding two black eyes behind a pair of dark glasses, which she explained with a panda-like smile,

> "I am really thrilled about the coaching award. After all, it took me five years to talk them into letting me take the test".

> "I was doing some coaching and was stupid enough to try jumping in hockey shoes. Still as I've been knocking high jump bars off for all these years, I suppose it's only fair that one should sit up and hit me back!"

Dorothy naturally specialised in high and long jump coaching, and served successfully progressing athletes at county, international and Olympic level in the 1960s and 1970s.

She was regularly in action for club sessions two or three times a week at the Carshalton track, at the famous and late lamented London University track at Motspur Park leading on to Surrey School Courses, and at Lilleshall nurturing specially selected young athletes on National Courses.

Innovatively, Dorothy set about learning ballet training under the expert tuition of ballet- master Andrew Hardy, while other coaches including Arthur Gold (later Sir Arthur), and hurdles star, Peter Hildreth, who became The Sunday Telegraph athletics correspondent, made notes to help widen their respective repertoires. Soon afterwards she and Gold invited the great Dame Margot Fonteyn and her regular partner "danseur noble" Michael Somes to Bisham Abbey where talent camps were being held. Both ballet stars warmed to the project and enthusiastically passed on their expertise. Dorothy was convinced of the benefit and as the great British coach Geoff Dyson had famously advised "She went away to her hinterland to spread the gospel".

Thus ballet exercises were soon introduced to her charges at Mitcham, many of whom, especially the girls, have happily recalled some of her dance-oriented sessions. Others more reticent, mostly male athletes, rather grudgingly conceded that while at the time rather red in the cheeks for more than one reason, their jumping had clearly benefited from the privations of pirouettes, the occasional pas-de-deux and even more stringent bar work!

Much in demand in the 1960s as a pioneer female who had broken into the former all-male preserve of AAA coaches, and uniquely armed with her ballet-enhanced routine, Dorothy enjoyed her new-found fame way beyond her beloved Mitcham club. On one such occasion, she travelled to Northern Ireland to spread the gospel. She was welcomed as a guest at the Belfast home of former British team mate, Thelma Hopkins.

Despite the warm hospitality of the friendly Anglo-Irish family, Dorothy was to coin a phrase, "her customary confident self", so much so that the atmosphere became more than a little tense. The situation seemed more than a little stressful for the younger Thelma and was fast getting out of hand when, with "feathers about to fly", Mrs Hopkins intervened. The wise mother of two highly-talented daughters had fortunately picked up the counter-productive vibes, and defused a potentially volatile situation, after which all was reported to have become sweetness and light. Looking back years later, Dorothy revealed her awareness of at times being difficult to deal with. "I don't do diplomacy", she confessed.

Son Barry was a responsive protégé, especially when it came to hurdling, and he progressed from the 1964 Surrey Schools Championships, winning the junior boys' title to gain county selection for the All England Schools Championships at the Copthall Stadium, Hendon. There facing the highest quality opposition, and inhibited by his limited stature he did not progress beyond the heats. Both he and his mother subsequently agreed that he was at a disadvantage when it came to leg length in the high hurdles event, and from then on he happily concentrated on his favourite sport of football. He excelled, going on to play for notable non-league sides Corinthian Casuals whose home ground was the Oval, and Tooting and Mitcham United nearer to home at Sandy Lane. He was offered a trial at Crystal Palace, but mother's wisdom prevailed and he was persuaded to continue his studies, finally settling for a rewarding career as a PE teacher.

Older brother David loved his football at local level, reserving his competitiveness for defending his corner in spats with his mother!

Dorothy was by then working as a technical official at big White City meetings, where she and the family would often link up with legends of the sport like Harold Abrahams, Fanny Blankers-Koen and Mary Rand. Her experience in the sport also led to her being invited to become a British selector.

Later, in 1967 Dorothy wrote "Teaching Athletics in School and Club", a concise coaching booklet which became one of the most popular publications of the Athletics Arena magazine educational handbooks, and which subsequently featured on many an athletic-minded P.E. teacher's shelf.

Dorothy's somewhat regimented Sunday morning coaching sessions, which continued like clockwork for many years, are generally remembered with appreciation by stars and journeymen alike, for most received a fair share of her time and expertise. They willingly endured the testing transition from scissors to straddle, from which Dorothy had been unable to benefit towards the end of her own competitive career. They didn't have the comfort of cushioned landing modules, but generally fell unceremoniously on to a heap of sand. More painfully following a failure, there were regularly inflicted red wheals from the "Toblerone-shaped" aluminium laths, which would then top the sand of those fairly distant times. This would surely have attracted the attention of present-day health and safety officials!

Near to home, Chris Brambley was one of three Mitcham A.C. athletes Dorothy coached, who all cleared 2.00m plus. He won three Surrey senior titles in 1974, 1975 and 1976 as well as taking the junior crown in 1975. A close rival of his, Paul Munt, was runner-up with a clearance of 1.90m at Motspur Park in 1975 and went on to work as a coach, carrying on in the Tyler tradition.

On the wider stage, notable among her many charges, some of whom competed for Great Britain in the Rome and Tokyo Olympics, were internationals Lorna Boothe, Jill Hall, Frances Slaap and Gwenda Matthews. Dorothy remained proud too, to have coached Eleanor Rowe - Britain's first female athlete to clear 6'00" (1.83m). Dorothy had in those days more often than not generously offered accommodation to top athletes in her care who lived beyond the London area. Still in touch until very recently from her new home in Australia, Eleanor recalled with gratitude her coach's contribution to her sporting career.

Many of the, dare one say, thicker-skinned athletes thrived on her regime, but others more sensitive, quietly moved on to pastures new, seeking a more personal and sophisticated approach. Mitcham AC athletes in disciplines not under Dorothy's jurisdiction viewed her with awe and some measure of unease, for she seldom spoke with them, leaving them disappointed at not having been given the Olympian's seal of approval.

Dorothy eased out of coaching on the creation of Sutton and District AC into which her beloved Mitcham AC disappeared. At the time, Bill Payne, the only Mitcham AC committee member voicing opposition to the proposed merger, clearly recalls from Canada Dorothy's "violent opposition" to the Mitcham/Sutton merger. For many weeks she continued to bombard him with her opposition at the Crystal Palace Recreation centre where they both coached on Sunday mornings way back then.

The Carshalton track, home of the Sutton and District AC, was duly refurbished and a plaque recognising those who had donated to the cause was mounted on the restaurant wall. Surprisingly, in the circumstances, the name Dorothy Tyler featured among them!

In 1968, the innovative Dick Fosbury sensationally stunned the athletics world, focusing eyes on the high jump when he won the Olympic gold, clearing the bar backwards with a height of 2.24m. The "Fosbury Flop" was well and truly born. Tyler's feathers were well and truly ruffled and her long and often voluble anti-campaign began. His style, she insisted, was "simply NOT high jumping!"[42]

Debbie Brill, a young Canadian jumper, had in fact perfected her own backwards technique, the "Brill Bend" a little earlier but Fosbury's Olympic success ensured it was his name that was to be immortalised in association with the technique. Brill was also dismissed by Dorothy, who referred to her "cheating her way to success". Brill was 30 years after Tyler's times and in some ways their careers ran parallel, although their personalities were very different. Both achieved teenage success, took the world record, and won two Empire/Commonwealth gold medals. Both of them had children and then returned successfully to the fray. But while Tyler was intense and traditional, Brill was very much a free spirit who never heeded Dorothy's advice to young athletes to "go to bed

---

42 *Dorothy's son Barry strongly supports his mother's views on the validity of the flop. He feels the new technique should be designated as a separate athletic discipline, with the previously long-established styles retaining their place.*

by 8pm until married". The two never met, but Brill much admired Tyler from afar for her achievements over so many years, but considered her funny for her "stick in the mud view of evolving techniques" and "maybe a bit straight laced".

Canute-like, Dorothy steadfastly refused to accept the inevitable tide of Fosbury followers, arguing that he and his kind were going against all that was involved in "honest" high jumping! "Going head first is a dive...". She would snarl, regularly raising the controversial subject with anyone who had a receptive ear.[43]

Clearly, even the progress which featured the Straddle technique must have irked her, for with sand landing pits being heaped up to accommodate landing on one's back, her Western three-point landing must have become more than tricky!

Maybe her feelings were strengthened by the fact that her retirement from top class athletics had taken place several years before. She had no chance to try the new technique, which, if known in her time, would surely have helped her to eclipse her already amazing achievements, first employing the good old schoolgirl scissors, before successfully making a tough transition to the Western Roll.

Dorothy didn't seem to take much satisfaction from having been the world's best at both techniques during her chequered career, and with time running out for her to take the next step to the straddle during the twilight of her competitive days, she had had to witness Britain's Sheila Lerwill straddling above her into the record books.

One can only guess what height Dorothy might have achieved had she been able to encompass the Fosbury technique during her distinguished career, but it is interesting to note that the

---

43 *It should be remembered that in Dorothy's early days as a high jumper there was a "no-diving" rule which made head first jumps illegal. This was rescinded because Western Roll and then straddle jumpers were going over the bar sideways and it is almost impossible to judge when the head went over first.*

women's world record has advanced 17cms since. Had the amalgamation of her club not taken place one can only speculate how long she might have continued coaching, maybe even to have eaten humble pie and moved on to the much maligned Fosbury Flop.

In 2008, Dorothy was the predictably outspoken Guest of Honour at a Sports Journalists' Association Awards Dinner, as a recipient of their prestigious Lifetime Achievement award. Princess Anne and Dick Fosbury were also present. Dorothy, unfazed, said dogmatically, "You can't go over the bar head first!" She was clearly wrong, but no-one took offence.

When she again met her high jumping "bête noir", Fosbury, during the UKA Conference at Loughborough in 2009, there was clearly tension, followed by a "frank exchange" of ideas, for Dick's wife Robin reported that "No punches were held!" Later Dick spoke glowingly of Dorothy as "such an incredible, legendary athlete who at 16, with no coaching and with no assistance won Olympic silver and repeated the feat 12 years later as a mother of two at the 1948 Olympic Games – an incredible feat". A fragile peace was then declared especially for a photo call, which Dorothy clearly relished, before she returned to her previous position as one of the most devoted disciples of "real" high jumping, not diving!

Dorothy, seldom a shrinking violet, especially when talking about her competitive days, was, however, much more reserved about her charitable and advisory contributions to the world of sport. She was, it has become apparent, instrumental in the development of a fair and democratic distribution of funds for the sadly short-lived Sportsmatch Scheme. Glynne Jenkins, one of its key co-ordinators, is fulsome in his praise of her involvement.

Dorothy was active too, away from athletics, working for several years helping with the rehabilitation of stroke victims through ballet therapy, delivering "Meals on Wheels" on a nearby estate, and latterly for several years, working as an assistant in her local Mind Charity shop.

The adopted "Olympic Auntie" to a primary school for disabled children in Bexhill, Dorothy continued to display great public spirit by answering numerous questions from inquisitive youngsters via their teacher well into her nineties.

In Olympic year, London 2012, the youngest girl athletes of Old Palace School of John Whitgift enjoyed a competition to design replacements for the covers for her 1948 London Olympic programmes, which may well have been "collected" by her sons. The winners Gaby Bailey, Kate Ferguson and Keya Patel, were absolutely thrilled at the prospect of meeting their Olympian "neighbour", to be shown her medals and to have their photograph taken with her.

Chapter 6
BITTER-SWEET MEMORIES

Dorothy was the most dedicated of Mitcham AC members until she found its assimilation into Sutton and District AC a pill too bitter to swallow. She continued to declare her great sadness at the loss of identity of a club with such a fine heritage. Mitcham colours were worn with distinction and pride by many fine athletes, Olympians among them, with Dorothy indisputably heading the distinguished field. She is closely pursued by fellow Olympian and European 1500m champion Brian Hewson, middle-distance star of the 1950s, at the fore of the Mitcham AC All-Time Top Ten, the rest of whom are:

3   Muriel Gunn-Cornell :-   80m hurdles and long jump, 31 internationals and a World long jump record
4   Anne Smith :- 1964 Olympian. 15 internationals and set World records at 1500m and 1 mile in the same race and also set a British 800m record.
5   Judy Vernon :- 1972 Olympian. 100m hurdles
6   Jenny Taylor-Pawsey :- 17 Internationals 1961-76, and member of World record 4 x 400m relay team, which clocked 3:37.6
7   Bevis Reid-Shergold :- 1948 Olympian Shot/Discus, 8 internationals and WAAA Champion 1948 & l949
8   Lorna Boothe:- Olympian, 1976 and 1989 100m hurdles. Commonwealth Champion
9   Andrea Lynch: - Olympian 1972 and 1976 100m and 4x100m
10 Barbara Burke :- 80m hurdles ,10 Internationals and a World Record for 80m hurdles 1936, WAAA champion 100m and 200m champion, 1936 and 1937. Won 80m hurdles at 1938 Empire Games competing for South Africa

Brian Hewson, now resident in South Africa, was fulsome in his praise of his senior club colleague, and said that it would be hard to find a more devoted member with such a high level of personal achievement. He went on to say that whenever possible, despite international commitments, Dorothy would sportingly turn out for the club, often competing in several events. Brian further speculated aloud that nowadays the athletics world would be unlikely to find such enthusiasm.

One can understand Dorothy's obvious disappointment at her club's disappearance, but it is so sad that the new generation of athletes in Sutton and District A.C. is totally unaware of the great heritage which she and others left them. Many of the Sutton club's trophies would not be there today, were it not for her achievements and generosity.

It would have been wonderful if, following the London 2012 Olympic Games, Dorothy could have been happily reconciled with the new club, and in particular its young members who have no axe to grind. They would be enthralled and inspired by her amazing athletic journey through school, club, county and country athletics participation which brought Commonwealth, European and Olympic medals and English Native, UK, Commonwealth, European, and World high jump records.

In retirement, Dorothy retained her avid interest in athletics, and tirelessly continued to contribute to the cause which she so loved.

As a respected team manager, the highlight for Dorothy was the responsibility invested in her in September 1965 with a trip behind the "Iron Curtain", where she led the British women against the might of the DDR (East Germany) in Berlin at the Friedrich-Ludwig-Jahn Stadium. Her strong team included both Olympic gold medal long jumper Mary Rand and Mary Peters, who later took pentathlon gold in the 1972 Munich Games.

On another occasion, when she led a small group of British women to an international meeting in Belgium, she faced a reasonably founded "mutiny" when the sprinters Maureen Tranter and Madeleine Weston refused to race on the indifferent grass track. One can imagine her pronouncing, "Grass was my favourite take off surface... I can't see what you are worried about". It is, however, reported that she did do no such thing, and stood up stoutly for her "refuseniks", and their decision not to compete.

In addition she was a founder member of The British Olympians, and in that role she attended the 150th anniversary of The Much Wenlock Games in July 2000. As if that were not enough, she graduated through the officials' ranks, establishing herself as an international judge and referee for field events.

Fifty years after her fourth and final Olympic competition, Dorothy did not quite recall her 1948 experience as she had originally been quoted. In the programme celebrating the anniversary of the London Games she was quoted as saying.....

> "As a matter of fact the high jump competition was completely overshadowed by the arrival of the men marathon runners in the stadium especially the cheers for Tom Richards[44], the Polytechnic Harrier, winning the silver medal. It was just the same back in Berlin with the marathon runners really disturbing the concentration of the high jumpers. I was so young and inexperienced then that I think it cost me the Gold medal in '36.......but never mind all that, so long ago. Isn't it marvellous that so many of us are still around today?"

Later when casting her memory back again to the 1952 Olympics, Dorothy likened the seemingly all-suffering, but totally dominant 10,000m gold medallist Czech Emil Zatopek, who had stormed home in splendid isolation in 29:59.6.

He also took gold in the 5000m and then made his debut in the marathon event where he yet again struck gold, having asked the non-plussed Briton, Jim Peters, "Are we going fast enough?" before heading off into the distance.

---

44 Tom Richards junior confirmed that his father, a one-time Mitcham AC member, was in fact a South London Harrier at the time of his London Olympic success.

Still feisty at 81 in 2001, and with a razor-sharp recall of envisaged injustices and slights, Dorothy was awarded a well-deserved MBE for services to athletics, presented by HRH Prince Charles. On that memorable occasion at Buckingham Palace, Prince Charles casually remarked, "You have been a long time coming!" to which she cheekily reposted, "Well, your Highness, you have been a long time asking!" .

Many thought and still believe that with her catalogue of great achievements during her long dynamic sporting and coaching career, which few could challenge, a more prestigious honour was merited. The redoubtable Dorothy had, it might be argued, a greater genuine claim to an OBE or even to being dubbed Dame, than some of the current incumbents.[45]

"I thought that it was the record high of my athletics career", she said, only to have doubts later when invited to the 60th Anniversary of the Sports Writers' Association to be honoured by their top award in recognition of 60 years of service in the sport. She felt even that was eclipsed when her induction to the England Athletics Hall of Fame was announced in 2009. It was Dorothy's hope that her grandchildren and great-grandchildren will in due course enjoy it and be suitably inspired.

True to form even at that prestigious occasion, Dorothy once again could not resist taking a poke at the (by her) much maligned "Fosbury Flop" technique. Seated next to Dame Mary Peters, she complained about its illegality, casting back to the controversy surrounding "Babe" Didrickson's relegation to second place in the 1932 Olympic high jump. Then, "Babe" had been jumping with a suspiciously low head position in her unique Western Roll style. Mary quietly pointed out that without the universal recognition of the Fosbury technique, she would not have won Olympic pentathlon gold at the Munich Games in 1972!

---

45 Dorothy herself had strong personal views on this subject!

Dorothy, the one-time "Golden Girl of Athletics", considered by many as "A Woman of Our Era" was never far from the limelight. One can speculate that she possibly featured in more press, radio and television interviews than any other sports personality.

Curiously, she never commented on the fact, that had not the War intervened, it is highly likely that her already legendary status would have had its bar raised mind-bogglingly, to that of a six-time Olympic athlete and maybe even a quadruple medallist.

When she finally retired from involvement in athletics, Dorothy became an enthusiastic golfer at the nearby Croham Hurst Golf Club, following husband Dick, who was already well established there. She developed a passion for the game which she would share with him for many happy years.

During one of her early sorties around the course, she was particularly intrusive, asking her partner what club he had selected at each hole until the 9th, when exasperated he said that one more such distraction and she would be on her own, while he would return to the bar for a soothing "sherbet". From then on a predominantly silent round improved in quality until the 19th was finally reached.

Dorothy was especially supportive of Dick in his year as club captain. As competitive as ever in her new found discipline, she was off a handicap of 18 in her first year. Before long, she had improved to an impressive handicap of 10 and scored a hole in one. At 80 plus, she won the Surrey title three times, and stunned many an opponent with her determination and quality of play, as evidenced in one particular match against considerably younger rivals from the Cuddington Golf Club. On that occasion Dorothy in her inimitable fashion distracted her opponents by telling them her life story during the 18 holes, which inevitably culminated in their defeat.

A senior member of Croham Hurst told me of one occasion

when Dorothy showed great compassion during a club tour to the Algarve. One of her friends had to return urgently to England because of her husband's illness. On hearing of this, Dorothy went round to her friend's bungalow with a bunch of flowers and said, "Don't worry about anything here; when it is time for us to return I will do all the tidying up for you. I will pack and bring anything back that you do not take now". Not only was she true to her word, but she also came back with presents for her friend's children.

She also conveyed mixed messages, often swinging from generous to scrooge-like behaviour in double-quick time. There was the instance of the fellow member who had lost a favourite driver. Dorothy with hardly a prod, generously offered one of hers on loan. After the match the borrower expressed her delight at the good round she had played with it. "Would you like to buy it?" Not surprisingly the answer was "Yes, please". When they failed to agree a price, it was decided the eager purchaser would take the wood to the Croham Hurst Professional for a neutral valuation. He suggested £80, but the friend then decided to play a trick on the hitherto philanthropic Dorothy, and stated tongue in cheek that £40 should do the deal. Dorothy's incredulous and irate reaction suggested that she knew the real value, but when her friend confessed, she calmed down and the deal was done.

When presented with several somewhat controversial and non-complimentary anecdotes about Dorothy from near contemporaries, it was deemed prudent to run them past son Barry.
"Didn't they tell you about mother's many solo sorties around the course on a buggy, when potential partners couldn't face her competitiveness?" he asked. That characteristic, linked with her lifelong ambition to win, had served her so well during her long career as an athlete. It had clearly remained with her, and was effective in some ways, but sadly failed to endear her within the more social side of golf.

On a different occasion, she told another club member that she had found her clearly marked ball in the rough beside the fairway. "I remember losing it somewhere on the approach to the 14th hole", the other woman responded, hoping for its return! "Very nice ball", Dorothy responded, calmly walking off with her "trophy".

For many years too, Dorothy was self-appointed Christmas tree provider and decorator for the Croham Hurst hall and reportedly did a very fine job at her own expense!

She and Dick supported many Dinner Dances at the club and had there been a championship for purchasing raffle tickets, Dorothy would surely have been well to the fore. Her apparent generosity in this context, was, however, somewhat diluted on one occasion when she scooped seven prizes, none of which was handed back for redraw and none of which was given to anyone seated at the same table!

Dorothy also became a devoted, if somewhat over-dogmatic, member of a bridge group at the Croham Hurst club. The other members could no longer tolerate her single-mindedness and hatched a cunning plot. On the due day, the conspirators told Dorothy that, sadly, due to the advancing years of all concerned this would be their final gathering. At the end of proceedings, a somewhat subdued Dorothy returned home in her routine taxi, oblivious of the fact that her erstwhile "friends" had arranged to re-convene the following week without her!

Dorothy was renowned for taking on the golf club fruit machine with a vengeance, spending much of her spare time there feeding it with far more money than the final jackpot would realise. Her determination to win was once clear to see for those present, who gave provenance to a four-hour marathon, until the keenly sought coins came crashing out.

When a 1936 Olympic Torch mysteriously appeared outside a charity shop in 2000 it was referred to Sothebys for valuation and subsequent auction. The company, having discovered that

Dorothy was a survivor from those Games, saw publicity potential in linking the "Grand Old Lady" with the sale. They contacted the family and it was arranged for Dorothy to be interviewed and photographed, after which the rare item was offered up for online sale. Very soon Dorothy decided that the torch should be hers, and in discussions with son Barry and his wife Sue it was agreed to bid on her behalf.

On the due day Dorothy was agitating to discover the outcome, but with Barry and Sue at work, and not being computer literate, she was forced to control her impatience for several hours. At the first opportunity and to his astonishment and delight, Barry discovered that the Tyler bid had succeeded.

The precious item soon became an item of self-promotion for Dorothy, who paraded and displayed it at the slightest opportunity. She even took it to London on more than one occasion in a Tesco bag, as a prop for media interviews. As time went by, she became quite careless over its security, regularly telling questioners that she kept it in the loft, more often than not adding that she slept with her Olympic silver medals under the pillow.

When former National Coach Tom McNab's play "1936" was performed at the Braithwaite Hall, Croydon in 2009, the stage was also set for Dorothy to appear as celebrity on the post-performance question and answer panel. Silver-haired, smart, sharp, and striking in a scarlet dress, she clearly reveled in her real life connection with Tom's thought-provoking production, which encompassed sport, politics, racism and intrigue. She reminisced and responded alike with enthusiasm, and proudly showed her high jump silver medal, and the Berlin Olympic relay torch, which Barry had succeeded in purchasing for her in a Sotheby's auction, to the audience. For its part, the audience was captivated by the old lady's recall of her participation in Hitler's Olympics some 60 years previously, as a wide-eyed but confident teenager.

In 2012, the author, while travelling in a mini-cab en route to an athletics event, was told by his driver that not long before he had driven an old lady who claimed to have been an athlete. She had, he said, shown him some very nice old coins! The warning bells sounded; Barry was notified, and her two Olympic silver medals were removed for security. Ever willing to express strong views, Dorothy, the Grand Old Lady of British Olympians, thought that the Olympic Games were too competitive and nationalistic. In addition, her view was that the opening and closing ceremonies were far too excessive. "Over the top and a waste of money!" she declared emphatically.

Her preferred opening would include the enactment of national ceremonies, in London's case The Ceremony of the Keys as held daily at the Tower, and a fly-past by the Red Arrows RAF display team. More controversially, she believed the parading athletes from the competing nations should not be allowed to take cameras or wave as they march! Such intrusions she felt diluted the sense of occasion.

Asked what advice she would offer any talented sixteen-year-old girl athlete, she said "Do what you want to do, try several events, keep at it and NEVER give up, and go to bed by 8 o'clock until you are married". Was the latter really serious advice from someone who when sixteen herself had challenged her chaperones' vigilance way back in 1936? I caught a glimpse of devoted husband Dick as this pearl of wisdom was delivered. His eyebrows certainly raised, and a suggestion of a smile crossed his knowing face, but never a word left his lips!

John Brett, sprinter and Mitcham AC teammate in the 1950s, kindly forwarded some informative correspondence from Dorothy, revealing some of the flattering demands placed on the "Grand Old Lady" of British athletics in her later years. In 2005, she wrote that the 100th Anniversary of the Olympic Committee[46] was keeping her very busy. A visit to Buckingham Palace received top mention to be followed by references to conferences, forums and television appearances.

---

46 British Olympic Association, which was formed in 1905.

She also helped an unnamed author working on a book about pre-war Germany. Almost as an aside, she included mention of her involvement in bridge, charity work and golf. In that particular letter she said "It broke my heart when Mitcham AC became Sutton and District. I joined in 1931 as an 11 year old". Clearly proud of her major representative achievements these too were mentioned, plus the interesting addition of her having set "12 Age World Records!"

Two letters sent to John four years later gave further insight into the life she and Dick were leading. They had just returned from an Arctic cruise incorporating Iceland and Norway during which she was delighted to have met a Mitcham AC man and friend of Brian Hewson, whose name she had frustratingly forgotten. She added that because of the cruise, she had been unable to accept an invitation to Berlin, and on the home front missed a lunch at the Imperial War Museum. "I am inundated with requests to talk about 1936 and 1948 to sports colleges and surprisingly the RSPCA!" she wrote. She did, however, manage to appear in a film, " The Outbreak" at The Eden Project in Cornwall about global warming. She "happened to let slip" too that she would be getting an award at a dinner in Birmingham...". But I am not allowed to talk about it!"

Six days later she wrote again, unsure whether she had replied to John. This time, she had remembered that the former Mitcham AC athlete, whom she had met on the cruise was one Terry Godwin. Probably in the context of John's letter, she added that she had seen quite a lot of Dick 'Phosby' (but we know whom she meant!).

In the last of these letters, sent in July 2011 she talks of two free tickets (clearly her allocation for the 2012 London Olympic Games), and that she would have the opportunity to apply for two more to purchase. At that time she added that she was taking a break from golf at the age of 91, because of a sciatic problem. A 2012 press cutting from John Brett showed that Dorothy had enthusiastically joined the campaign to protect what remained of the old News of the World track built in

1924, near Canons and Park Place, where Mitcham AC and other club athletes had trained before and after World War II.

Chapter 7
ONCE MORE INTO THE LIMELIGHT

The 2012 London Olympics were fast approaching, and this living legend of athletics was still much in demand from the media for her reminiscences and opinions. She was also among the privileged contributors to sport, who were nominated to take part in the torch relay. Delighted to be considered, but ever the realist, she saw the task to be tackled unaided as unrealistic, often saying "I can't run 400m at my age". This despite being assured more than once that she would be allowed to walk. She never received a response from the organisers to her request for help.

A more tangible opportunity for Dorothy to be acknowledged in the 100 days before the Games emerged when co-founder London Marathon, John Disley, himself an outstanding Olympian, invited her to act as celebrity starter for the great event. Would she accept? Of course she would! ...well not quite!!

The thrill of potential involvement remained with her, but clearly that did not prevent her from expressing a surprisingly critical opinion of the event organisers. "They should have asked me years ago!" was the grumpy response, when the subject was broached. "They've asked far too many odd people over the years!"

When prominent personalities such as Princess Diana and Terry Waite were mentioned, the flow of discontent slowed. Virgin entrepreneur Richard Branson got short shrift for having sportingly dressed up as a fairy when he started the race in 2011. "What a silly man!" she asserted.

"Well maybe I'll do it, but I certainly won't dress up as a fairy". It soon became subject to certain conditions of course, practical rather than financial, and only deserved by such a unique senior citizen, would have to be met!

"Will they provide a door-to-door taxi?"

"Could Dick and maybe Barry go too?"

"And what about food, drink and toilets?"

she queried with more interest. A phone call from John Disley, reassuringly pointed out that all concerned would be suitably fed and watered, and seated within easy reach of toilet facilities. With the promise of a luxury cab too, all Dorothy's "demands" were met and the deal was done!

"I've been selected...I've been selected" was the greeting I received when I called on one of my many visits to the Tyler home later that spring day. "Surely not for the high jump?" I joked. Like an excited, newly selected young international, Dorothy revealed her news, and Dick's accompanying smile indicated a shared delight.

Late into the evening Dorothy was still finding it hard to control her well-understood excitement, although she remained adamant that she would not even think about following in the fancy-dress footsteps of her predecessor, Sir Richard Branson. At that moment I felt sure that the 30,000 plus marathon aspirants would be efficiently sent on their way, under possibly the world's most senior starter ever, who would certainly undertake her duties with the professionalism of one honed through three quarters of a century of very special sporting involvement.

Answering a pre-race questionnaire for the Virgin sponsored event's website, Dorothy expressed her pleasure,

> " I am thrilled to have been asked, especially in this Olympic year....it is an honour and gives me the chance to get back into athletics after not having been involved for quite some time....it's such a great event...I just hope I can press the hooter properly!"

Everything unravelled really well. The invitation included Dick and Barry. Prior to their departure, Dorothy, obviously prepared for the occasion with due respect having proudly donned one of her Olympic blazers, and not dressed Branson fashion, was outside her house early, but confused due to her evolving dementia. Barry, alert to the situation, took her inside to await the car and settle down for the events ahead. Once on her way, Dorothy amazingly went into totally acceptable performance mode. Barry was much relieved at her success at completing good interviews with both Sue Barker on BBC TV and John Inverdale on the radio. During the television interview, Dorothy, hardly a shrinking violet, appeared to revel in it, and even took the opportunity to advertise her "forthcoming book" which she was writing!

Then with the help of her son, Dorothy eagerly climbed up to the starters' platform where she carried out her duties impeccably, thanks to some judicial prompting from her son. The process was tiringly repeated four times, once for each, with Dick prudently nodding off elsewhere.

She absolutely loved the massed start and thrilled especially at the significant participation of women in the event. Her 1950s pioneering spirit was very evident on this great occasion.

Soon the trio, accompanied by John Disley, were whisked away in a convoy with police outriders to Trafalgar Square, and thence by buggy to the finish in the Mall. By then the old folk were understandably tired but happy to have had such a memorable experience and were eternally grateful to their son for his support.

Returning to the relative calm of home at Ridge Langley, it was then off to their regular Sunday tea at the golf club where she enjoyed the bonus of congratulations as numerous members had seen her TV interview that morning.

Later, Dorothy repaid her son's care and attention by giving him her tickets for the final day of the London Olympics at Stratford to see her specialism, the high jump.

Chapter 8
HOW HIGH WILL THE BAR RISE?

With the exception of the huge crowd response, the 2012 London Olympics was very different from Berlin 1936. One can only speculate as to what Dorothy would have made of the competition, in which all the competitors employed the "cheating Fosbury Flop technique" and all the twelve finalists cleared 1.89m with winner Anna Chicherova sailing over 2.05m.

Remember that the first three in Berlin in 1936 had shared the same height of 1.60m. By the next Olympics in London in 1948, Dorothy again shared the same height of 1.68m as the winner Alice Coachman (USA), but had to settle for a second silver medal. The 1948 jumpers were then 21cm below the 2012 back markers.

It was surprising to learn, that even after all her years as an athlete, coach and official, Dorothy's favoured surface for high jump take-off remained well prepared grass, which was the case when she set her world record of 5' 5 $^3/_8$" (1.66m) at Brentwood on 29th May 1939.

Dorothy was still an inspiration to many, among them Alice Coachman, who sent her a personally signed copy of her biography "Queen of the Track"[47] (2012) bearing the inscription "For Dorothy. You inspire us all to keep dreaming BIG and jumping high".

In a rare surviving copy of the journal of the now defunct "Whip and Carrot Club" for specialist high jumpers in 1955, Dorothy spoke out strongly against the hazards of built-up landing areas, expressing her preference for the predictable sand pit! Definitely a dinosaur with good reason, she wrote an article entitled "built up pits" a conflict of terms on a par with the

---

47 *Written with Heather Lang*

Epsom Downs. "Built up pits – I've met 'em. No thank you...". There then followed a catalogue of injuries she and other athletes suffered because of them. "....I now no longer jump where I know there are built up pits".

Long gone now are the days of such techniques as Scissors, Western Roll, Eastern Cut Off and Straddle. With Dick Fosbury cocking a snook at tradition in 1968, they all eventually went out of the window, and much to Dorothy's disgust were replaced by the head first over the bar technique. Nowadays, hugely expensive soft elevated landing areas are essential with many women routinely coming down head and shoulders first from over 2m, and men from over 30cm higher.

Although having complained personally to Dick Fosbury about his alleged innovation in high jump technique, Dorothy can at least be grateful to him and the other backwards jump pioneer Debbie Brill of Canada, for leaving her prowess as a scissor jumper and latterly Western Roll exponent relatively unchallenged in the record books.

Who knows when the next trail blazer of high jump technique will emerge to raise the bar even further? Dorothy herself feared that anything might have happened after the acceptance of Fosbury's "Illegal head-first" technique in 1968. "They might even succumb to two foot take-off jumping", she added as a parting shot! Somehow I think not!

......but the ever forward-thinking foreword writer Dick Fosbury, not averse to crystal ball gazing himself, sees adaptation of technique a distinct possibility as it was in Debbie Brill's and his day. Such a development could raise the men's record, currently standing at 2.45m (8' 0 ½") by Cuban Javier Sotomayor to the extraordinary elevation of 2.50m or more.

There is of course the possibility of the high jump finding its own Usain Bolt and then the Fosbury technique could still retain its place. The current crop of high jump exponents is rich in talent as evidenced by the fact that three of them set

160

personal bests of more than 2.40m in 2014. Currently top is Mutaz Essa Barshim of Qatar who achieved 2.43m, followed by Ukraine's Bohdan Bondarenko at 2.42m and Russian Ivan Ukhov with 2.41m outdoors and 2.42m indoors. There have been several unsuccessful attempts at a world record height, which suggests the record must be under serious threat.

As for the women, more relevant in this context, there is currently not the same apparent threat to the record. With most of the top performers in 2014 approaching the end of their careers the most likely threat would seem to be Maria Kuchina of Russia, who attained 2.01m indoors, but she is still 4% shy of the existing record. However, with the prospect of the 2016 Rio Olympics one hopes that a new generation will emerge to grasp the nettle. The British outdoor record holder, Isobel Pooley, who soared over 1.96m at Eberstadt in Germany to be ranked 14th in the world could be inspired. When asked to predict who would be the first woman to clear 2.10m there was no hesitation. She replied "Me!"

Modern women high jumpers owe much to Debbie Brill of Canada, to whom the "broad shouldered Fosbury" gives credit as the pioneer of the "backward" technique. Most people understandably attribute the advance to him, thanks to his Olympic triumph at the 1968 Mexico Games. Two years prior to that, Brill had introduced the style at the age of 14, and notably at 16, she became the first North American woman to clear 6' (1.83m). Remember, Dorothy was similarly precocious, having scissored over 5' 5" (1.65m) at the same age over 30 years earlier. West German jumper Ulrike Meyfarth became the first female to set a "Flop" world record, when she employed it for her 1.92m leap, which won her gold at the 1972 Munich Olympic Games, and equalled Austrian Ilona Gusenbauer's existing record. That provided a big hint as to what high jump treats were in store. Straddling briefly regained record ground during the next four years, courtesy of Bulgarian Yordanka Blageova (once), and Rosie Witchas, later GDR (four times), who between them progressed the bar to the peak of women's straddle jumping, with Ackermann achieving the magic 2.00m mark in 1977 when she improved the mark by 3cm in Berlin.

The Fosbury technique regained the record in 1978 through Sara Simeoni of Italy and then Meyfarth, who regained the record after a gap of ten years. The Flop now reigns supreme, with the current record set in 1987 by Stefka Kostadinova (Bulgaria) standing at 2.09m.

Chapter 9
TEA FOR THREE

Towards the end of June 2013, I realised with sadness that my privileged time with Dorothy had almost come to an end. I put two very similar remaining questions to her, on the Tylers' long and devoted relationship.

"Dorothy, I have a question for you ...".

"When you and Dick were courting, were there any challengers, any other handsome athletes whom you had noticed?"

The old lady thought for a moment or two...

"I am an athlete you know!" she replied with conviction.

"Dorothy, may I have a cup of tea please?"

"Do you take sugar?" she queried

"No thanks, I don't" I replied with my routine response.

Soon we were enjoying cups of her positive brew, and passing the time of the day.

On my next visit I thought I would try my question once more, but in a slightly different form.

"Dorothy, when you and Dick were courting, did any other good looking fellow catch your eye?"

Dorothy thought long and hard... "I'm a millionaire you know!" she replied cheerfully.

Women high jumpers around the world, eat your hearts out.

Here's a happy lady!

> "You're very lucky, Dorothy. May I have a cup of tea please?"

> "Do you take sugar?" she asked politely

> "No thanks, I don't"

Soon Dorothy, Dick and I were enjoying afternoon tea together, with the customary chocolate digestive biscuits.

> "It was no contest!" Dick whispered discreetly.

POSTSCRIPT

Dorothy's fascinating story lives on, delivered passionately by proud son Barry, in lectures and less formal talks, to amazed audiences and equally riveted individuals.

Dorothy and Dick finally left their Sanderstead home in late 2013 for residential care at Melford Court in East Anglia near Barry and his family's home. There, they were content and well cared for. In gratitude, Dorothy promised all the staff at the home a copy of "Thanks, No Thanks to Mr Hitler". At Melford, she had plenty of opportunity to parade her MBE. She did though, continue to maintain the view that an OBE would have been much more appropriate, and latterly expressed the view that elevation to the status of Dame should have been hers.

Dorothy died on 25th September 2014, and sadly she only saw drafts of this book which were happily given her nod of approval.

Appendix A
MAJOR RESULTS

High Jump Results

Olympic Games (British athletes shown)

1936	2nd	Dorothy Odam 1.60	9=	Nellie Carrington 1.50		
1948	2nd	Dorothy Tyler 1.68	6th	Bertha Crowther 1.58	8th	Dora Gardner 1.55
1952	2nd	Sheila Lerwill* 1.65	4th	Thelma Hopkins 1.58	7th	Dorothy Tyler 1.55
1956	2nd	Thelma Hopkins 1.67	12=	Dorothy Tyler 1.60	16=	Audrey Bennett 1.55

*Sheila Lerwill née Alexander

European Championships

1950	1st	Sheila Alexander 1.63	2nd	Dorothy Tyler 1.63	5th	Bertha Crowther 1.55

Empire Games (later Empire and Commonwealth Games, now Commonwealth Games)

1938	1st	Dorothy Odam 1.60	2nd	Dora Gardner 1.575		
1950	1st	Dorothy Tyler 1.60	2nd	Bertha Crowther 1.60	4th	Dorothy Manley 1.524
1954	1st	Thelma Hopkins 1.675	2nd	Dorothy Tyler 1.60	4th	Sheila Lerwill 1.575

Thelma Hopkins represented Northern Ireland, all others

represented England.

Empire Games heights are converted from feet and inches.

GB Internationals – sometimes the team competed as England, or were just England

1936	Blackpool	1st	Dorothy Odam 1.625	5th	Mary Milne
1937	Wuppertal	1st	**Dorothy Odam 1.62**		
1937	Krefeld	1st	**Dorothy Odam 1.62****		
1937	Brussels	1st	**Dorothy Odam 1.61**		
1939	Berlin	2nd	**Dorothy Odam 1.65**	5th	Dora Gardner 1.55
1949	FRA/NED	1st	**Dorothy Tyler 1.66**	4th	Dorothy Manley 1.45
1950	FRA	1st	**Dorothy Tyler 1.65**	2nd	Sheila Alexander 1.59
1951	IRE/SCO	1st	**Dorothy Tyler 1.65**		
1951	FRA	1st	Sheila Alexander 1.575	2nd	**Dorothy Tyler 1.575**
1952	ITA	1st	**Dorothy Tyler 1.63**	2nd	Thelma Hopkins 1.63
1953	NED	1st	Sheila Alexander 1.625	2nd	**Dorothy Tyler 1.575**
1954	SCO	1st	**Dorothy Tyler 1.52**	2nd	Maureen Hudson 1.50
1954	FRA	1st	**Dorothy Tyler 1.60**	3rd	Jennifer Frazer 1.473
1954	HUN	1st	**Dorothy Tyler 1.62**	2nd	Thelma Hopkins 1.60
1954	CS	2nd	**Dorothy Tyler 1.63**	3rd	Thelma Hopkins 1.63
1955	FRG	1st	Thelma Hopkins 1.69	2nd	**Dorothy Tyler 1.625**
1955	HUN	1st	Thelma Hopkins 1.70	2nd	**Dorothy Tyler 1.625**

1955	FRA	1st	Dorothy Tyler **1.59**	2nd	Audrey Bennett 1.56
1955	USSR	1st	Thelma Hopkins 1.70	2nd	**Dorothy Tyler 1.65**
1955	CS	1st	Thelma Hopkins 1.71	3rd	**Dorothy Tyler 1.66**
1956	HUN	1st	Thelma Hopkins 1.70	2nd	**Dorothy Tyler 1.62**

** The Krefeld high jump was originally won by Dora Ratjen with a World Record (see above for why it didn't stand!). The height Dorothy cleared is variously given as 1.61, 1.615 and 1.62.

WAAA Championships

	1st	2nd	3rd
1935	Mary Milne 1.55	**Dorothy Odam 1.524**	Dorothy Cosnett 1.47
1936	**Dorothy Odam 1.53**	Nellie Carrington 1.524	Alice Flack 1.50
1937	**Dorothy Odam 1.635**	Dora Gardner 1.60	Dorothy Cosnett 1.55
1938	**Dorothy Odam 1.575**	Dora Gardner 1.575	Dorothy Cosnett 1.55
1939	**Dorothy Odam 1.65**	Dora Gardner 1.575	Barbara Lovelock 1.525 Dorothy Cosnett 1.525
1945	Dora Gardner 1.525	**Dorothy Tyler (Odam) 1.525**	Doris Endreweit 1.475
1946	Dora Gardner 1.55	Doris Endreweit 1.525	Bertha Crowther 1.525
1947	Gladys Young 1.55	Bertha Crowther 1.50	Sheila Alexander 1.50
1948	**Dorothy Tyler 1.625**	Bertha Crowther 1.60	Gladys Young 1.525
1949	**Dorothy Tyler 1.60**	Sheila Alexander 1.60	Bertha Crowther 1.60
1950	Sheila	**Dorothy Tyler 1.60**	Joan Cowan

			1.575
1951	Sheila Lerwill 1.72 WR	**Dorothy Tyler 1.60**	Ursula Hynes 1.525
1952	**Dorothy Tyler 1.65**	Sheila Lerwill 1.65	Thelma Hopkins 1.625
1953	Sheila Lerwill 1.65	Thelma Hopkins 1.65	**Dorothy Tyler 1.60**
1954	Sheila Lerwill 1.625	**Dorothy Tyler 1.625**	Thelma Hopkins 1.575
1955	Thelma Hopkins 1.65	**Dorothy Tyler 1.625**	Audrey Bennett 1.60
1956	**Dorothy Tyler 1.60**	Mary Bignal 1.60	Jean Pearce 1.60

WAAA Indoor Championships

	1st	2nd	3rd
1935	Mary Milne 1.50	Nellie Carrington and **Dorothy Odam 1.47**	
1936	Mary Dumbrill (Milne) and **Dorothy Odam 1.57**		E Spencer 1.50
1937	**Dorothy Odam 1.59**	Alice Flack and Dora Gardner 1.47	
1938	**Dorothy Odam 1.55**	Alice Flack 1.525	E Spencer 1.47
1939	**Dorothy Odam 1.55**	J Arnold 1.525	Doris Endreweit 1.50

Women's Area Championships - South

1935	**Dorothy Odam 1.57**	1936	**Dorothy Odam 1.65**
1937	**Dorothy Odam 1.535**	1938	**Dorothy Odam 1.60**
1939	**Dorothy Odam 1.66**	1945	**Dorothy Tyler 1.56**
1946	Dora Gardner 1.55	1947	Gladys Young 1.55
1948	**Dorothy Tyler 1.625**	1949	**Dorothy Tyler 1.60**
1950	Sheila Alexander 1.60	1951	Sheila Lerwill 1.675
1952	**Dorothy Tyler 1.60**	1953	**Dorothy Tyler 1.60**
1954	**Dorothy Tyler 1.575**		

High Jump Records

At the start of Dorothy's career the World Record stood at 1.65m which was achieved by both Jean Shiley and Mildred Didrikson during the 1932 Olympics. In fact both cleared 1.67m in a jump-off, but Didrikson was then ruled to have dived. 1.67m did not count as a World Record because it was during a jump-off. In 1933 Dora Greenwood of UK jumped 1.65m but it was not ratified as a World Record.

5 Aug 1935	Chiswick	1.60	UK Junior Record (5' 3") *breaking 1.58 set by Phyllis Green in 1927*
1 Jun 1936	Brentwood	1.65	equal World Record but not ratified (5' 5") also UK and Junior Record
10 Jun 1936	Blackpool	1.63	This was reported in the press as a British Record. Dorothy noted it as such on the back of a photograph. Did she have reason to doubt the Brentwood mark?
29 May 1939	Brentwood	1.66	World Record (but not recognised until 1957)
7 Aug 1948	Wembley	1.68	UK Record (and personal best) shared Olympic record (also cleared 1.66m on first attempt which equalled her own record)
15 Jun 1957	London	1.676	Not listed in all records, but possible V35 record (Built-up shoe)

Other Events

Long Jump

1937 Brussels International Match	2nd (5.10) - also in relay team that took 3rd place
1950 Empire Games	8th (5.09)

1951 Ireland/Scotland International Match	2nd (5.30)
1951 France International Match	1st (5.40)
1954 Empire and Commonwealth Games	11th (5.06)
WAAA Championships	1st in 1951 (5.58), 3rd in 1952 (5.23)
Southern Championships	1st in 1950 (5.24)
Headed 1951 rankings with 5.73m	

Javelin

1950 Empire Games	4th (32.85)
1954 Empire and Commonwealth Games	5th (32.93)

80 metres Hurdles

1950 Empire Games	4th in Heat, one place from final

Pentathlon

WAAA Championships 1951	1st with UK Record 3224 points (3953 with 1954 tables)

Club Competitions

As a stalwart of Mitcham AC in the pre-league days, Dorothy remained very proud of the fact that she helped her club in both the Atalanta Trophy (won 3 times, and 2nd once) and the Norrkoping Trophy (also won 3 times, 2nd 5 times, and 3rd 4 times).

Appendix B
TEENAGE HEADLINES

"NEW GIRL STAR OF THE SPORTS FIELD"

"CHAMPION AT 15—AND A HIGH AND LONG JUMPER"

"THE TEST IS TODAY" (1935)

"BRITISH GIRL HIGH-JUMPER HAS A PROBLEM THAT WILL TAKE SOME GETTING OVER....SHE AIMS TO CLEAR HER OWN HEIGHT"

"MISS ODAM'S FEAT EQUALS WORLD HIGH JUMP RECORD IN BERLIN"

"HIGH JUMP SHE IS A HE - SO DOROTHY GETS A WORLD RECORD"

"DOROTHY'S TITLE WAS HELD BY A MAN"

Appendix C
HOUSEWIFE HEADLINES

"MOTHER'S FINE HIGH JUMP"

"MOTHER OF TWO IS OLYMPIC HOPE"

"MOTHER JUMPS TO IT"

"NOW DAD MINDS THE BABY AS MOTHER JUMPS FOR RECORD" (1949)

"A LOT OF FUSS ABOUT NOTHING" - MRS. DOROTHY TYLER (1950)

"PENTATHLON TRIUMPH DOROTHY TYLER AGAIN"

"HOUSEWORK KEEPS THIS HIGH JUMPING QUEEN FIT"

"MOTHER OF TWO CAN JUMP HER OWN HEIGHT"

"I HATE HOUSEWORK INSISTS REBEL CHAMPION"

"HIGH JUMPING HOUSEWIFE"

"HIGH JUMP MOTHER CHAMPION MOTHER TRAINS SONS"

"DOROTHY TYLER THE LEAPING HOUSEWIFE"

"I'LL BET MUM WILL BE TOP"

"DOROTHY'S THIRD TRIP TO GAMES"

"DOROTHY'S THIRD EMPIRE TRIP"

"MRS TYLER GOES ON THIRD TRIP" (1954)

"MRS TYLER, BRIAN HEWSON SECOND AT VANCOUVER" (1954)

"MOTHER TOTES UP WINNINGS"

"MRS TYLER IS BACK-AND WINS A TITLE"

"DOROTHY TYLER OUT JUMPS SHEILA LERWILL"

"OLYMPIC ATHLETE MOTHER"

"THE REMARKABLE HOUSEWIFE FROM MITCHAM"

"EVERY YEAR IS A LEAP YEAR FOR DOROTHY"

"YET ANOTHER TITLE FOR MRS TYLER"

"MRS TYLER MOVING TO CROYDON" (1956)

"MOTHER MEANS TO WIN AT THE OLYMPICS"

"WIFE WITH AN OLYMPIC HOPE"

"BRITAIN'S HIGH JUMP DEBT TO DOROTHY TYLER" (1957)

"MUM SCORES DOUBLE WIN - AT 39"

"THE GIRL WHO KEPT JUMPING" 1959

"DOROTHY TYLER WINS THE HIGH JUMP"

"AAAMAZING"

"SKETCH HELPS TO FIND MEDAL WINNER DOROTHY" (1960)

"AFTER 18 YEARS, DOROTHY IS A CHAMPION"

"SHE'S A WORLD CHAMP 18 YEARS LATE"

"NEVER TOO OLD TO BE A CHAMPION AGAIN"

"DOROTHY TYLER CAN COACH MEN ATHLETES"

"QUEEN OF THE HIGH JUMP SHE'S A WORLD CHAMP"

"PRESIDENT, MRS TYLER SETS A PRECEDENT"

"TYLER STEALS THE SHOW"

"DOROTHY RUNS 84 SEC LAP AT 50"

"A HIGH JUMP HEROINE, HER BRUSH WITH HITLER AND A SKIMPY KNICKER SCANDAL"

"DOROTHY JOINS THE GREATS" 2009 ENGLAND ATHLETICS HALL OF FAME

"I SEWED MY UNIFORM TO WEAR IN 1936" (2001)

"IT WAS THE YOUTH OF THE WORLD GETTING TOGETHER"

"THEY CALLED UP BIG BEEFY AMAZONS"

"TYLER JUMPS TO DEFEND OLD FASHIONED VALUES"

"DOROTHY TYLER IS TOUCHING DOWN - ON A GOLF COURSE"

"OLYMPIC LEGEND IS STILL FULL OF SPIRIT AND FLAIR" (2008)

"TYLER STEALS THE SHOW" (2008)

"TYLER SENDS FOSBURY FOR THE HIGH JUMP!" (2008)

"I SEWED MY UNIFORM TO WEAR IN 1936" (2010)

"OLYMPIC LEGEND IS STILL FULL OF SPIRIT"

Appendix D
THE TECHNICAL EVOLUTION OF HIGH JUMPING

High jump has, over the years seen more obvious changes in technique than any other athletic event. Integral to these changes has been the pursuit of perfection involving the economy of effort in projecting the body most efficiently over the bar. Progressive changes have incorporated body movements which have placed the position of the athlete's centre of gravity lower in the clearance phase. Thus less effort is required to succeed at any height, than would have been used with an earlier technique.

Simplistically, the progression has been from Scissors to Fosbury Flop, with the key intermediate styles being Eastern Cut-Off, Western Roll and Straddle. The Scissors jump, with its straight run up and characteristic leg kicks, was used in both standing and running jump competitions, and is still used as a warm-up component by many present-day athletes. The last men's world record to be set using Scissors was 1.93m in 1887 by W Byrd Page, but he was using a modified version of the true Scissors technique.

Eastern Cut-Off

The Eastern Cut-Off was developed by Michael Sweeney of New York Athletic Club, who used it to set a World Record in 1895. Originally referred to as the "Sweeney Style", it is a significant development from the Scissors technique where the body is more horizontal, and the jumper twists in the air, landing facing the bar. The jumper's centre of gravity is closer to the bar than for a Scissors jump, thus rendering it more efficient, as the jumper's centre of gravity can be closer to the ground. It is interesting that descriptions of Sweeney's run-up could replicate that of a modern "flopper".

There were several variations of the Eastern Cut-Off of which the most notable is probably that of Clinton Larson (USA), who had an extremely fast run-up and went over the bar on his back, although the back was parallel to the bar. His best of 6' 9½" (2.07m) in 1920 exceeded the world record but did not count because it was during an exhibition. Both the Scissors and Eastern Cut-Off have many variations, and it has been said that "the number of different high jump styles is the same as the number of high jumpers".

Western Roll

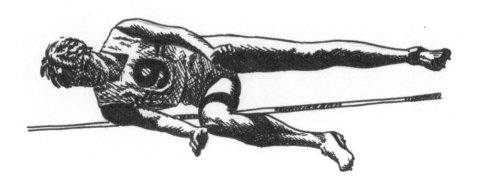

The Western Roll was developed by George Horine of Stanford, and used to break the World Record in 1912. Although it was originally described as the Horine Style, the names Eastern Cut-Off and Western Roll soon became standard, reflecting the great rivalry between the two sides of the USA. It was a few years before it started to be adopted by jumpers on the East Coast of the USA, so even at the 1936 Olympics European and Japanese jumpers favoured the Eastern Cut-Off. The take-off is from the foot nearer the bar in contrast to the Scissors jumpers who use the outside foot, so a Scissors jumper converting to Western roll would find it easier to approach from the other side. The jumper goes over the bar on their side with the lower knee bent, and with the upper shoulder rotating forward during the clearance, enabling the hands to be used for the landing in conjunction with the leg that was uppermost during clearance. This all brings the centre of gravity closer to the bar and, accordingly, greater heights can be achieved than for the Eastern Cut-off.

Straddle

The Straddle is a development of the Western Roll, where with more rotation the jumper goes over the bar face down (belly roll), bringing the centre of gravity even closer to the bar. The invention of the Straddle is often credited to Jim Stewart in 1930, and Dave Albritton became the first World Record Holder using the Straddle technique in 1936. Initially, Straddle jumpers used the generally slow run-up of the Western Roll, but over time they became faster.

Until the 1930s there was a "no diving" rule in high jump, which banned jumpers from going over the bar head first, and also said that the head must not be below the hips at the moment of clearance. This was repealed around 1936 because it was clear that some Western Roll (and Straddle) jumpers were going over the bar with the head just in front of the rest of the body. Judging this was subjective - Mildred "Babe" Didrikson was disqualified in the final of the 1932 Olympics during the jump-off, but she felt there was no difference from any of her other jumps. In 1936 both Cornelius Johnson and Dave Albritton, joint World Record Holders and the first two in the Olympics, were extremely marginal on the rules as they were then. The rules were then simplified to just requiring a one-footed take-off, but it is unlikely the legislators realised they were inadvertently opening the door to more extreme styles, leading eventually to the Brill Bend and Fosbury Flop. Before those styles were introduced, Straddle jumpers took advantage of the new rules and the "Dive Straddle" came in. It is credited to Gilbert (Gil) Cruter (USA), who called it his "barrel-roll" technique, and was then developed in the early 1950s by a group of Swedish jumpers, before being perfected by the Soviets in the early 1960s under their legendary coach Vladimir Dyachkov. Arguably the finest exponent of the Straddle was Valeriy Brumel, who reigned supreme from 1961 to 1963 with 6 world records to his name in that period.

It took some time for the different techniques to spread around the world, so at the 1936 Olympics most men were using a form of Eastern Cut-Off, with the Americans using the Western Roll and Straddle. At the same time most top women stuck to the Scissors - one obvious exception was Mildred "Babe" Didrikson. It was only after the war that Dorothy really started losing out to Western Roll (Alice Coachman) and Straddle (Sheila Alexander). Iolanda Balas with her Eastern Cut-Off style was the one jumper to buck the trend.

Fosbury Flop

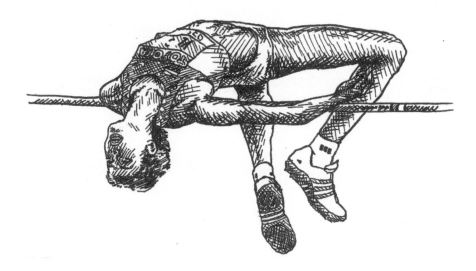

The Fosbury style, now universally accepted despite Dorothy's protestations, ticks all the boxes within the current rules and technical awareness. With its J or reversed J shaped approach, and with the most efficient conversion of momentum from the horizontal to the vertical, it allows the greatest speed at take-off, and it critically achieves the lowest possible height of the athlete's centre of gravity to the bar during clearance. Debbie Brill's technique, which she developed independently, used a straighter run up. The name "Flop" may have come from the movements of a fish as it is landed, but it may also have initially come from a journalist's description which was not meant to be complimentary.

Another key factor in high jumping evolution has been the advance over years from landing on grass, followed by raked sand, to heaped sand, and finally the luxury graded foam modules which are in use today, costing many thousands of pounds. The use of foam started at the same time as Dick Fosbury and Debbie Brill evolved their unique styles; previous jumpers that might have headed the same way would have been discouraged by the prospect of landing in sand. Also worthy of note is the fact that the current jumpers clearing far superior heights to their predecessors drop similar distances on to a more comfortable surface.

The best heights achieved in each technique by males and females are listed below.

MALE			FEMALE		
Scissors					
Historically uncertain. Modern jumpers have cleared over 2.10m with the scissors in training and warming up			Fanny Blankers-Koen (Netherlands)	1943	1.71m
Eastern Cut Off					
Kalevi Kotkas (Finland)	1936	2.04m	Iolanda Balas (Romania)	1961	1.91m
Western Roll					
Gene Johnson (USA)	1966	2.17m (indoor)	Zheng Fengrong (China)	1957	1.77m
Straddle					
Vladimir Yaschenko (USSR)	1978	2.35m (indoor)	Rosie Ackermann (GDR)	1977	2.00m
Fosbury Flop					
Javier Sotomayor (Cuba)	1993	2.45m	Stefka Kostadinova (Bulgaria)	1987	2.09m

Such was Dorothy's amazing inherited physique that she could virtually get her head and torso at the level of her leading leg during the clearance of the bar. Her record suggests that, shorter for instance than Fanny Blankers-Koen, she was one of, if not THE most technically efficient scissors jumpers ever.

Mental ambition and flexibility led to her moving on to the Western Roll, but with time not on her side, she really did astonishingly well to make the top ten when using it in the 1952 Olympics. The way in which Dorothy was able to maintain similar heights as she got older might suggest that she was still learning how to get the best from her new technique, and once again questions what she might have achieved had she switched sooner. Other far younger athletes in her day were able to hone the style to a level of perfection more quickly.

The lanky Iolanda Balas (6' 1", 1.85m tall) with fourteen world records to her name was certainly the Eastern Cut Off exponent from whom to learn, while the powerful Straddle jumper Valeriy Brumel, who set six men's world records, was clearly the one to mirror in the early 1960s. Rosie Ackermann (née Witchas) with seven world records was the most successful straddler, delaying the inevitable march of the floppers.

Following the innovative Olympic success of Dick Fosbury in 1968, high jumping took the "backward leap" forward into what became the most successful phase of the event's fascinating history.

Illustrations for Appendix D by Alice Chandler

Appendix E
DOROTHY'S SEASONS BESTS
1934 TO 1963

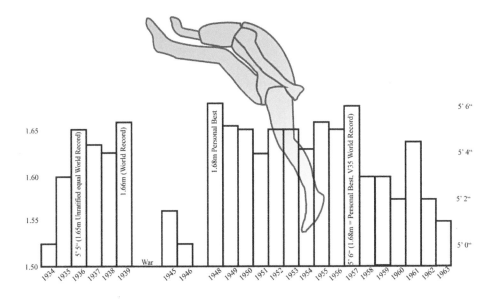

Comparison to World Best

	World	Dorothy		World	Dorothy
1934	1.606	1.524	**1946**	1.65	1.524
1935	1.612	1.60	**1947**	1.65	
1936	1.651	1.651	**1948**	1.68	1.68 (=1st)
1937	1.635	1.635	**1949**	1.657	1.657
1938	1.64	1.625	**1950**	1.692	1.651
1939	1.66 (WR)	1.66	**1951**	1.72 (WR)	1.625

1940	1.651		**1952**	1.67	1.66
1941	1.66		**1953**	1.69	1.651
1942	1.65		**1954**	1.73 (WR)	1.63
1943	1.71 (WR)		**1955**	1.71	1.66
1944	1.65		**1956**	1.76 (WR)	1.66
1945	1.59	1.562			

Appendix F
IMPERIAL / METRIC CONVERSION

Heights have been given in the units of each competition, where this is known. In high jump, heights are usually given to the nearest ¼ inch or 1 cm (0.01m), but some lists give conversions from imperial to the nearest millimetre (0.001m) or 5mm (0.005m).

Imperial	Metric equivalent (to nearest 1cm)	
5' 0"	1.52m	
5' 1"	1.55m	
5' 2"	1.57m	
5' 3"	1.60m	
5' 4"	1.63m	
5' 5"	1.65m	World record that Dorothy equalled - unratified
	1.66m	Dorothy's 1939 world record
5' 6"	1.68m	Dorothy's personal best in competition 1948 & 1957
5' 7"	1.70m	
6' 10"	2.09m	Current women's world record (set in 1987)

Appendix G
ARCHIVE DOCUMENTS

WOMEN'S AMATEUR ATHLETIC ASSOCIATION.
FOUNDED 1922.

Feb. 10th 1936

Dear *Miss Golam,*

You have been recommended by the W.A.A.A. committee as a "possible" for the Olympic Games team.

Will you therefore ~~reply~~ answer the enclosed questionaire and return same to me at your earliest convenience.

Yours sincerely,

Muriel A. Cornell

Hon. Secretary.

Selection letter as a "possible" for the 1936 Olympic Games

Telephone
KENSINGTON 2202
(4 LINES)
Telegrams
'OVALTINUS · PHONE
LONDON
Cable Codes
A.B.C. 5TH EDITION
MARCONI
INTERNATIONAL
WESTERN UNION
(5 LETTER)

A. WANDER LIMITED
Manufacturing Chemists

184, QUEEN'S GATE
LONDON, S.W. 7.

Works Laboratories & Farms
KING'S LANGLEY
HERTFORDSHIRE (L.M.S.)
Managing Director
Sir Harry Hague

Also at
BERNE
PARIS · MILAN
PETERBOROUGH, CANADA
CHICAGO
ALEXANDRIA
JOHANNESBURG
SYDNEY
WELLINGTON
COLOMBO
CALCUTTA
BOMBAY

Ref: .... C/U.U.

Miss D.Odam,
9, Edenvale Road,
Mitcham.

March
6th
1936

Dear Madam,

At the request of Mrs. M. Cornell, of the
Women's Amateur Athletic Association we are sending
you herewith a copy of the book entitled "Teaching
and Training Athletes" by Captain F.A.M. Webster.

We are also forwarding under separate cover a
large tin of "Ovaltine" in order that you may use
this product during your training for the Olympic
Games. The value of "Ovaltine" is fully demonstrated
in the book we are sending you, and we shall be only
too happy to send you a further supply of "Ovaltine"
on request.

yours faithfully,

p.p. A. WANDER LTD.

Leviol. C. Davison

Publicity Manager.

Olympic sponsors letter from A Wander (makers of Ovaltine)

MITCHAM ATHELTIC CLUB.

Affiliated to A.A.A., W.A.A.A., S.C.A.A.A., S.C.C.A., S.C.W.A.A.A., S.T.C.C.A. & W.H.S.A.

SURREY RELAY CHAMPIONS 1927, 1935.   WINNERS OF SURREY YOUTH'S RACE 1926/27/28/29 the 1930, 1933.
SOUTH OF THAMES SENIOR CROSS COUNTRY CHAMPIONSHIP, 1935.
SOUTH OF THAMES JUNIOR CROSS COUNTRY CHAMPIONSHIP 1930, 1934.

HON. GEN. SECRETARY:
W. G. BATEMAN,
Roxford, 34, Crowborough Road,
Tooting, S.W.17.
(To whom ALL correspondence should
be sent unless otherwise stated).

Founded  1920.

HON. TREASURER:
J. S. LEWIS, Esq.,
68, Bickersteth Road, Tooting, S.W.17.

Asst. Hon. Gen. Sec.:
A. G. PAWSEY,
64, Rostella Road,
Tooting, S.W.17.

President: F. H. PRIEST, Esq.
Founder & Life Vice-Pres.: S. H. COLEMAN, Esq.
Headquarters: "WHITE HART" HOTEL, MITCHAM.

Hon. Section Sec. :
F. W. PRIEST, Esq.

37, Newbolt Avenue,
Cheam,
Surrey.

11. 6. 36.

Dear Miss Odam,

At a meeting of the Ladies Track Committee
last evening I was instructed to convey to you their
hearty congratulations on your two successes on Tuesday,
firstly for winning the International High Jump, secondly
and most assuredly for breaking the British record
for High Jump by clearing 5ft. 4ins. it is indeed
pleasing to realise that we have such fine athletes as
yourself in the Mitcham Athletic Club, and that when
you are competing you are bringing honour and glory to
the club as well as personal honour.

Assuring you of our best wishes for your
future successes we should like to know what you
were going to be the second member of the Mitcham Athletic
Club to break a world's record another 1½ inches would
just do it. anyway heres hoping.

Yours sincerely,

[signature]
Hon. Track Sec.

Mitcham AC (Ladies Track committee) congratulations letter
after she set British record at Blackpool

MITCHAM ATHELTIC CLUB.

Affiliated to A.A.A., W.A.A.A., S.C.A.A.A., S.C.C.C.A., S.C.W.A.A.A., S.T.C.C.A. & W.H.S.A.

SURREY RELAY CHAMPIONS 1927, 1933.   WINNERS OF SURREY YOUTH'S RACE 1926/27/28/29 tie 1930. 1933.
SOUTH OF THAMES SENIOR CROSS COUNTRY CHAMPIONSHIP, 1935.
SOUTH OF THAMES JUNIOR CROSS COUNTRY CHAMPIONSHIP 1930. 1934.

HON. GEN. SECRETARY:

W. G. BATEMAN,
" Roxford," 34, Crowborough Road,
Tooting, S.W.17.
(To whom ALL correspondence should
be sent unless otherwise stated).

Founded   1920.

HON. TREASURER:

J. S. LEWIS, Esq.,
68, Bickersteth Road, Tooting, S.W.17.

Asst. Hon. Gen. Sec.:
A. G. PAWSEY,
64, Rostella Road,
Tooting, S.W.17.

President: F. H. PRIEST, Esq.
Founder & Life Vice-Pres.: S. H. COLEMAN, Esq.
Headquarters: "WHITE HART" HOTEL, MITCHAM.

Hon. Section Sec.:
F. W. PRIEST, Esq.

Vice-Presidents:
Sir R. J. MELLER,
 J.P., M.P.
I. H. WILSON, Esq.,
 J.P.
N.   ALLEN, Esq.
J. BARRETT, Esq.
S. J. HART, Esq.
Dr. G. BROWN,
ELLIS BURTON, Esq.
MRS. ELLIS BURTON.
E. J. CHAPPELL, Esq.
H. CHANDLER, Esq.
R. COLE, Esq.
G. W. COLE, Esq.
S. H. CORNELL, Esq.
E. COLVIL, Esq.
F. C. CRAFFORD, Esq.
J. C. CRUMP, Esq.
O. S. DANBY, Esq.
H. C. DENYER, Esq.
W. T. DESMOULINS, Esq.
J. ELLIS, Esq.
E. J. D. FIELD, Esq.
Mrs. C. M. FOSBURY.
W. FROST, Esq.
J. E. GILLMAN, Esq.
A. R. GREEN, Esq.
C. D. GRIFFIN, Esq.
E. GROVER, Esq.
F. W. GUNN, Esq.
H. HANN, Esq.
G. HASTINGS, Esq.
B. HEAL, Esq.
H. HOWES, Esq.
D. C. HICKS, Esq.
R. LENFESTEY, Esq.
H. J. LOVATT, Esq.
H. E. MARTIN, Esq.
E. H. NEVILLE, Esq.
J. OWEN, Esq.

23rd June, 1936.

Dear Miss Odam,

At the meeting of the Management Committee
of the above club held on Friday last I was
instructed to convey to you the Committees congratulations
on your performance in creating a new British Record
at the International match at Blackpool.

Yours sincerely,

W. G. Bateman

Hon.-Gen. Secretary.

Another congratulations letter from Mitcham AC Management Committee

195

THE BRITISH OLYMPIC ASSOCIATION

THE XIth OLYMPIAD
BERLIN, 1936.

Book of Instructions
Dates of Competitions
Lists of Competitors
AND
Tables of Metric Equivalents

Cover of the 1936 Olympic athletes' handbook

MESSAGE TO GREAT BRITAIN'S TEAM RECEIVED FROM HIS MAJESTY THE KING.

I send my best wishes to the members of the British team taking part in the forthcoming Olympic Games, where I am sure that they will maintain the tradition of British Sportsmanship.

EDWARD R.I.

Buckingham Palace.
August 1st, 1936.

HIS MAJESTY KING EDWARD VIII.
Patron of the British Olympic Association.

Camera Portrait by Hugh Cecil, London.

A message from the King in the 1936 Olympic athletes' handbook

ATHLETICS—(Men).—*Continued.*

COMPETITORS.—Men.

E. Boyce.	A. G. Pilbrow.
A. G. K. Brown.	J. V. Powell.
J. A. Burns.	J. H. Potts.
F. Close.	B. L. Prendergast.
J. F. Cornes.	G. L. Rampling.
N. H. Drake.	W. Rangeley.
W. E. Eaton.	L. Reavell-Carter.
T. Evenson.	A. V. Reeve.
D. O. Finlay.	W. Roberts.
J. Ginty.	D. M. Robertson.
R. Graham.	J. Sheffield.
F. R. Hadley.	A. W. Sweeney.
E. Harper.	J. St. L. Thornton.
C. B. Holmes.	G. T. Traynor.
J. Hopkins.	P. D. Ward.
T. Lloyd Johnson.	F. R. Webster.
R. K. I. Kennedy.	S. R. West.
B. F. McCabe.	W. H. Whitlock.
J. L. Newman.	C. A. Wiard.
A. J. Norris.	F. F. Wolff.
A. Pennington.	S. C. Wooderson.

ATHLETICS—(Women).

OFFICIALS.

Mrs. M. A. Cornell ...	...	...	...	*Team Manager*
Mrs. C. Palmer	...	...	...	*Chaperone*
Mrs. R. Taylor	...	...	...	*Masseuse*

COMPETITORS.

A. Brown.	D. Odam.
B. Burke.	V. Olney.
N. Carrington.	K. Tiffen.
I. Chambers.	V. Webb.
K. Connal.	G. Whitehead.
E. Hiscock.	

8

Great Britain's Olympic Team, 1936.

(The Address in Berlin, when known, is given in brackets, except for those staying in the Official Residences.)

President, British Olympic Association:

THE LORD PORTAL, D.S.O., M.V.O. (Adlon Hotel).

Members of International Olympic Committee:

THE LORD ABERDARE ... ... } Adlon Hotel
THE LORD BURGHLEY, M.P., Commandant of Team }
SIR NOEL CURTIS-BENNETT, K.C.V.O. ... }

Headquarters Staff:

EVAN A. HUNTER, O.B.E. ... ... *Secretary*
CAPT. L. H. CHURCHER ... ... *Housing Officer*
P. F. CRANMER ... ... }
K. S. DUNCAN ... ... } *Assistants*
L. A. PIRIE ... ... }
MISS O. A. SHALE ... ... }
ALAN GRAVES (Rheinbabenallee 49 Dahlem) ... *British Attaché*
CAPT. VON USZLAR-GLEICHEN ... ... *German Attaché*

ATHLETICS—(Men).

OFFICIALS.

A. S. TURK ... ... }
W. J. PEPPER ... ... } *Team Managers*
DR. A. ABRAHAMS ... ... *Medical Officer*
F. WRIGHT ... ... }
E. S. STORRIE ... ... } *Masseurs*
E. J. HOLT (c/o Strey, Berlinerstr, 158) ... }
H. H. NEVILLE (Esplanade Hotel) ... } *Nominated as*
W. J. PALMER (Littaur, Neve Kanstr 17) ... } *Federation*
C. W. F. PEARCE (c/o Strey, Berlinerstr, 158) ... } *Officials*
J. W. TURNER (Russischer Hof) ... }
H. M. ABRAHAMS (Russischer Hof) ... }
W. R. MILLIGAN (Russischer Hof) ... } *Member of*
CAPT. T. D. MORRISON ( ) } *International Board*

7

List of competitors in Athletics from the 1936 athletes' handbook

HOCHSPRUNG FRAUEN High jump, women
Gant en hauteur, dames

Weltrekord: 1,65 m, J. Shiley (USA) 1932 — Olymp. Rekord: 1,65 m, J. Shiley (USA) 1932

Olympia - Siegerinnen

1928	Catherwood	Kanada	1,59 m
1932	J. Shiley	USA	1,65 m

15.00 Uhr

Entscheidung

51 Stevens, Catherine	87 Bell, Mary Margaret	736 Rogers, Annette
Belgien	Canada	USA
308 Koopmans, Jantina	38 Carter, Doris Jessie	307 Koen, Francina Elsje
M₃	Australien	Holland
Holland	858 Kaun, Elfriede	224 Leissner, Alice
175 Lipasti, Irja	Deutschland	Frankreich
Finnland	284 Odam, Dorothy	394 Nishida, Junko
283 Carrington, Nellie	Großbritannien	Japan
Großbritannien	776 Kelly, Kathlyn	775 Arden, Alice J.
11 Lanitis, Ismène	USA	USA
Griechenland	859 Ratjen, Dora	426 Stefanini, Zulejka
507 Nowak, Wanda	Deutschland	Jugoslawien
Oesterreich	225 Nicolas, Marguerite	717 Csák, Ibolya
	Frankreich	Ungarn

Teilnehmer nach Startfolge geordnet

Olympia-Siegerin 1936

....

2..   3..

4..   5..

6..

Der Hochsprung geschieht über eine dreikantige Latte, die auf glatten Auflege-
platten zwischen Sprungständern liegt.
Gemessen wird von dem tiefsten Punkt der Oberkante der Latte in lotrechter Rich-
tung bis zum Erdboden.
Abwerfen der Latte oder unausgeführter Sprung, bei dem aber der Springer den
Boden verläßt oder jenseits des Sprunggestells berührt, bewirkt, daß der Versuch
zwar gezählt, aber nicht gewertet wird. Desgleichen gilt es als Fehlsprung, wenn
ein Bewerber seitwärts springt und dabei die senkrechte Ebene unter der Latte
passiert.
Wenn zwei oder mehr Teilnehmer beim Hochsprung die gleiche Höhe erreichen,
wird ein weiterer Versuch auf die nicht übersprungene Höhe gestattet. Führt dieser
Versuch zu keinem Ergebnis, so soll die Latte auf die vorher übersprungene
Höhe gelegt und ein weiterer Versuch gestattet werden. Die Latte soll dann so
lange höher oder tiefer gelegt werden, bis das Stechen entschieden ist.

8

The Women's High Jump page from the 1936 Berlin Olympic
programme

MITCHAM ATHLETIC CLUB.

Affiliated to A.A.A., W.A.A.A., S.C.A.A.A., S.C.C.C.A., S.C.W.A.A.A., S.T.C.C.A. & W.H.S.A.
SURREY RELAY CHAMPIONS 1927, 1933.   WINNERS OF SURREY YOUTH'S RACE 1920/27/28/29 tie 1930, 1933.
SOUTH OF THAMES SENIOR CROSS COUNTRY CHAMPIONSHIP, 1935.
SOUTH OF THAMES JUNIOR CROSS COUNTRY CHAMPIONSHIP 1930, 1934.

HON. GEN. SECRETARY:

W. G. BATEMAN,

" Roxford," 34, Crowborough Road,

Tooting, S.W.17.

(To whom ALL correspondence should
be sent unless otherwise stated).

Founded 1920.

HON. TREASURER:

J. S. LEWIS, Esq.,

68, Bickersteth Road, Tooting, S.W.17.

Asst. Hon. Gen. Sec.:
A. G. PAWSEY,
64, Rostella Road,
Tooting, S.W.17.

President: F. H. PRIEST, Esq.
Founder & Life Vice-Pres.: S. H. COLEMAN, Esq.
Headquarters: "WHITE HART" HOTEL, MITCHAM.

Hon. Section Sec.:
F. W. PRIEST, Esq.,

Vice-Presidents:
Sir R. J. Meller,
  J.P., M.P.
I. H. Wilson, Esq.,
  J.P.
M. D. Allen, Esq.
J. Barrett, Esq.
S. J. Bartlett, Esq.
Dr. G. Brown.
Ellis Burton, Esq.
Mrs. Ellis Burton.
E. J. Chappell, Esq.
H. Chandler, Esq.
R. Cole, Esq.
G. W. Cole, Esq.
S. H. Cornell, Esq.
H. E. Colvil, Esq.
F. C. Crafford, Esq.
J. C. Crump, Esq.
O. S. Danby, Esq.
H. C. Denyer, Esq.
W. T. Desmoulins, Esq.
J. Ellis, Esq.
E. J. D. Field, Esq.
Mrs. C. M. Fosbury.
W. Frost, Esq.
J. E. Gillman, Esq.
A. R. Green, Esq.
C. D. Griffin, Esq.
E. Grover, Esq.
F. W. Gunn, Esq.
H. Hann, Esq.
G. Hastings, Esq.
B. Heal, Esq.
H. Howes, Esq.
D. C. Hicks, Esq.
R. Lenfestey, Esq.
H. J. Lovatt, Esq.
H. E. Martin, Esq.
E. H. Neville, Esq.
J. Owen, Esq.
G. H. Penn, Esq.
W. J. Pepper, Esq.
F. C. Richards, Esq.
F. C. Roden, Esq.
H. Searle, Esq.
C. G. Simmonds, Esq.
Dr. P. M. Turnbull,
  M.C.
S. H. Varndell, Esq.
A. H. Williams, Esq.
W. D. Willison, Esq.
Mrs. T. Witherden.
T. Witherden, Esq.

21st August, 1936.

Dear Miss Odam,

      At the meeting of the Management
Committee of the above club held last evening I
was instructed to convey to you the Committee's
appreciation of your performances in the Olympic
Games and in Cologne.

      We all feel that you kept the
Mitcham A.C. flag flying in Germany and hope you
will continue with your successes.

      Yours sincerely,

W. G. Bateman

Hon. Gen. Secretary.

Letter of congratulations from Mitcham AC after the 1936
Olympics

Life Membership of Mitcham AC. 1936

ORIENT LINE

England · Australia   S.S. ORMONDE

Christmas Day, 1937.

SIR JAMES and LADY LEIGH-WOOD send greetings to the teams from England, Scotland, Wales and Northern Ireland, and wish a Happy Christmas to all.

AT this Festive Season there will be much generous hospitality, and Sir James trusts he will not be misunderstood when he expresses the hope that all concerned will *"go slow"* so as not to impair their training in view of the serious work ahead.

Christmas Day greeting to the England team on board the SS Ormonde

202

Sydney 150th anniversary celebration certificate

Programme cover for ISTAF meeting in Berlin 1939, one of
the last meetings before the war. The meeting is now part of
the Diamond League

Form 178.

ROYAL AIR FORCE.

PHYSICAL TRAINING ~~AND DRILL~~
INSTRUCTOR'S CERTIFICATE.

Certified that 447740 LACW. TYLER, D.J.B.

completed a full course of Physical Training ~~and Drill~~

~~which included the rudiments of Boxing, Swimming,~~

~~Fencing, Gymnastics~~ and the Organisation of Games,

and obtained a Satisfactory standard of efficiency.

Percentage of marks 67

Grading of Certificate "B"

P. Hollick Flt/o   Officer i/c

~~Commandant,~~

W.A.A.F. Course

~~No. School~~ of Physical Training

~~and Drill,~~

Royal Air Force.

Date 6.10.43.

(*11854) Wt. 53608—3566 1,000 4/43 T.S. 700

PE Instructors' Certificate

BRITISH AMATEUR ATHLETIC BOARD

Hon. Secretary J. C. G. CRUMP   Hon. Treasurer H. M. ABRAHAMS

CROWN CHAMBERS, 118 CHANCERY LANE, LONDON, W.C.2

Celebrations of the XIVth Olympiad

LONDON, 1948

The British Amateur Athletic Board has selected

Mrs. Dorothy J. Tyler,

to represent GREAT BRITAIN in the

High Jump

for the Olympic Games to be held at Wembley
Stadium, London, from July 29th to August 7th, 1948.

Jack C. G. Crump

Hon. Secretary.

London Olympic Games selection certificate

THE BRITISH OLYMPIC ASSOCIATION

THE XIVth OLYMPIAD
LONDON, 1948

List of Great Britain's Competitors

Instructions to Team

Dates of Competitions

AND

Tables of Metric Equivalents

London 1948 Olympics Athletes' Handbook cover

Athletics (Men)—*Continued*

D. D. MACKENZIE
H. A. MARTINEAU
A. McCORQUODALE
S. H. McCOOKE
E. McDONALD BAILEY
H. E. A. MOODY
C. J. MORRIS
R. A. MORRIS
G. W. NANKEVILLE
J. NESBITT
H. A. OLNEY
H. J. PARLETT
A. S. PATERSON
R. C. PAVITT
J. H. PETERS
M. W. PIKE

M. D. POPE
D. C. PUGH
L. REAVELL-CARTER
T. RICHARDS
W. ROBERTS
H. G. TARRAWAY
G. D. C. TUDOR
R. T. UNSWORTH
P. H. VALLE
A. WATT
F. R. WEBSTER
R. A. WEST
C. T. WHITE
G. B. R. WHITLOCK
H. WHITTLE
D. G. WILSON

ATHLETICS (Women)

(3 Officials, 20 Competitors)

OFFICIALS

MRS. W. E. HUGHES	... *Team Manager*
MRS. C. LESLIE...	*Asst. Team Manager*
... ...	... ... *Masseuse*

COMPETITORS

MISS D. BATTER
MRS. M. BIRTWHISTLE
MISS S. CHEESEMAN
MISS G. CLARKE
MRS. B. CROWTHER
MISS M. ERSKINE
MISS D. GARDNER
MISS M. GARDNER
MRS. W. JORDAN
MISS L. LEE

MISS K. LONG
MISS D. MANLEY
MISS M. PLETTS
MISS B. REID
MRS. J. SHEPHERD
MISS D. TYLER
MISS J. UPTON
MISS M. WALKER
MISS E. WHYTE
MISS A. WILLIAMSON

BASKET BALL

(3 Officials, 13 Competitors)

OFFICIALS

J. A. CLAY	... *Team Manager*
W. BROWNING	... *Assistant Team Manager*
A. W. RICHARDS	... *Masseur*

8

London 1948 Olympics Athletes' Handbook, Competitors Page

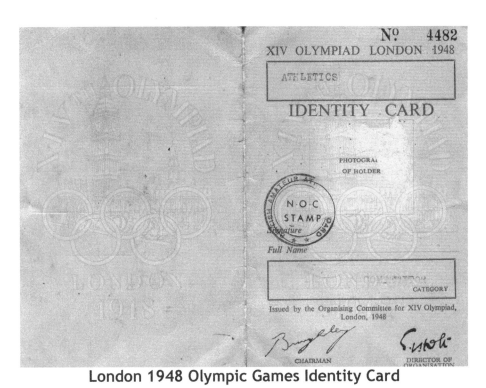

London 1948 Olympic Games Identity Card

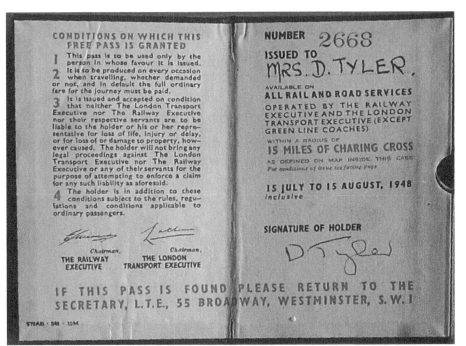

London 1948 Olympic Games travel pass contents

HIGH JUMP
WOMEN'S FINAL
SAUT EN HAUTEUR   SALTO DE ALTURA

3.35 P.M.

EVENT

4

Olympic Winners

		ft. in.	m.			ft. in.	m.
1928	E. Catherwood Canada	5 2¼	1.59	1932	J. Shiley U.S.A.	5 5¼	1.65
	1936 I. Csak Hungary	5 ft. 3 in.	1.60 m.				

World Record :   5 ft. 7¼ in.   1.71 m.   F. E. Blankers-Koen (Holland) Brentwood, 1943
Olympic Record : 5 ft. 5¼ in.   1.65 m.   J. Shiley (U.S.A.) and M. Didrikson (U.S.A.)
Los Angeles, 1932

The competition will start at 1.30 m, and continues at 1.40 m, 1.50 m, 1.55 m, 1.60 m and 1.65.

COMPETITORS

738	Beckett, V. R.	*Jamaica*	746	Iversen, A. M. R.		*Denmark*
692	Blankers-Koen, F. E.	*Holland*	753	Ludwig, Milly		*Luxembourg*
752	Bourkel, C.	*Luxembourg*	748	Ostermeyer, M. O. M.		*France*
676	Clara Muller, E.	*Brazil*	700	Phipps, C. L.		*Jamaica*
755	Coachman, A.	*U.S.A.*	754	Reed, E.		*U.S.A.*
747	Colchen, A. M.	*France*	740	Robinson, C. B.		*U.S.A.*
734	Crowther, B.	*Great Britain*	749	Ruas, S.		*France*
743	Dredge, D. M.	*Canada*	745	Silburn, K. E.		*Canada*
925	Gardner, D. K.	*Great Britain*	665	Simonetto de Portela, N.		
744	Gordon, S.	*Canada*				*Argentina*
751	Gyarmati, W. O.	*Hungary*	742	Steinegger, I.		*Austria*
			750	Tyler, D. J.		*Great Britain*

OLYMPIC CHAMPIONS 1948

1st	755	1.68	m.	5	ft	6⅛	in.	R
2nd	750	1.68	m.	5	ft	6⅛	in.	R
3rd	748	1.61	m.	5	ft	3⅜	in.	
4th	738		m.	5	ft	7¼	in.	
5th	743		m.	5	ft	2⅛	in.	
6th	734		m.	5	ft	2⅛	in.	

London 1948 Olympic Games programme. Event page.

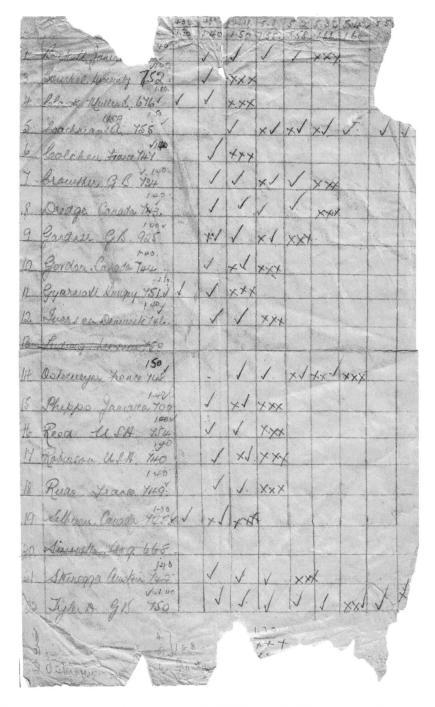

Handwritten results of the 1948 Olympic Women's High Jump
Transcript of the results

No	Name	Country	1.30	1.40	1.50	1.55	1.58	1.61	1.64	1.66	1.68	1.70
738	Beckett V.R.	Jamaica	-	o	o	o	o	xxx				
692	Blankers-Koen F.E.	Holland	DNS									
752	Bourkel C.	Luxembourg	-	o	xxx							
676	Clara Muller E.	Brazil	o	o	xxx							
755	Coachman A.	USA	-	-	o	xo	xo	xo	o	o	o	xxx
747	Colchen A-M.	France	-	o	xxx							
734	Crowther B.	Great Britain	-	o	o	xo	o	xxx				
743	Dredge D.M.	Canada	-	o	o	o	o	xxx				
925	Gardner D.K.	Great Britain	-	xo	o	xo	xxx					
744	Gordon S.	Canada	-	o	xo	xxx						
751	Gyarmati W.O.	Hungary	o	o	xxx							
746	Iversen A.M.R.	Denmark	-	o	o	xxx						
753	Ludwig M.	Luxembourg	DNS									
748	Ostermeyer M.O.M.	France	-	-	o	o	xo	xxo	xxx			
700	Phipps C.L.	Jamaica	-	o	xo	xxx						
754	Reed E.	USA	-	o	o	xxx						
740	Robinson C.B.	USA	-	o	xo	xxx						
749	Ruas S.	France	-	o	o	xxx						
745	Silburn K.E.	Canada	o	xo	xxx							
665	Simonetto N.	Argentina	DNS									
742	Steinegger I.	Austria	-	o	o	o	xxx					
750	Tyler D.J.	Great Britain	-	o	o	o	o	o	xxo	o	xo	xxx

1948 Olympic High Jump for Women, Full Results – Transcript of Handwritten Sheet

Notes:

Sports-Reference.com has first time failures at 1.64m and 1.66m for Alice Coachman, but the results shown here are consistent with both the Organising Committee Official Report and Harold Abrahams' press report.

The handwritten sheet shows Emma Reed of USA clearing 1.50m, but other sources say she only cleared 1.40m.

WOMEN'S AMATEUR ATHLETIC ASSOCIATION
FOUNDED 1922

Cross-Country Hon. Sec.
C. W. LEWIS, Esq.
37 Station Road,
Marston Green, Birmingham.

Hon. Coaching Organiser
MRS. M. CORNELL,
33 Mitcham Park, Mitcham, Surrey.
MITcham 3804.

President . . . The Right. Hon.
THE COUNTESS OF DERBY

Chairman . . . R. TAYLOR, Esq.

Publicity Hon. Secretary
W. HITCHIN, Esq.
9 Manor Road, ~~~~~ Kent.

Hon. Treasurer
MRS. C. PALMER,
The Datcha, 112 Edgwarebury Lane,
Edgware, Mddx.   EDGware 0489.

Hon. Secretary
MRS. W. E. HUGHES,
13 Selcroft Road, Purley, Surrey.
UPLands 1566.

October 1 th 1949.

Dear Mrs. Tyler,

EMPIRE GAMES, NEW ZEALAND, 1950.

At a meeting of the International Sub Committee of the above Association held yesterday you were selected to represent England in the following events:

High Jump, Hurdles, Long Jump and Javelin

I should be glad if you could let me know at your very earliest convenience whether you can accept the invitation. I should perhaps make it quite clear to you that this invitation is provisional and depends on whether the Empire Games Appeals Committee succeed in raising sufficient funds to meet the very great expense involved in transporting and equipping the team.

The team will leave England about the middle of December and will leave New Zealand about the beginning of March which means that the ship will arrive back about the second week in April. All travelling expenses will be met and uniform will be provided. If you are accepting the invitation I should be glad if you could let me know in your reply your height and also chest measurements, as these are urgently needed for the firm manufacturing the Track Suits.

Further the Committee make the request that if you are accepting you do not take part in any sport likely to cause injury such as Hockey, Net Ball or Lacrosse.

Yours sincerely,
Winifred E Hughes.
HON. SECRETARY.

Selection letter for the 1950 Empire Games

BRITISH EMPIRE GAMES

Auckland, New Zealand

1950

BOOK OF INSTRUCTIONS

DATES OF COMPETITIONS

Names of Teams from

ENGLAND, SCOTLAND and WALES

1950 Empire Games Athletes' Handbook cover

BRITISH EMPIRE GAMES

AUCKLAND 1950 NEW ZEALAND

ATHLETICS

FIRST DAY

SATURDAY, 4th FEBRUARY

AT

EDEN PARK

OFFICIAL PROGRAMME

19

50 Empire Games Programme cover

THE BRITISH AMATEUR ATHLETIC BOARD

(Affiliated to the I.A.A.F. as the governing Athletic Association for the United Kingdom of Great Britain and Northern Ireland)

Constituent Members:

THE AMATEUR ATHLETIC ASSOCIATION

SCOTTISH AMATEUR ATHLETIC ASSOCIATION

NORTHERN IRELAND AMATEUR ATHLETIC ASSOCIATION

PRESIDENT:

H.R.H. THE DUKE OF EDINBURGH, K.G.

Hon. Secretary: J. C. G. CRUMP

Clerk to the Board: G. W. SMITH

Hon. Treasurer: H. M. ABRAHAMS

Telephone: HOLborn 4795

Telegrams: ATHLETE, ESTRAND, LONDON

CROWN CHAMBERS
118 CHANCERY LANE
LONDON W.C.2

22nd June, 1952.

Dear Mrs. Tyler,

As President of the British Amateur Athletic Board, I am writing to you on its behalf to inform you that you have been selected to represent Great Britain and Northern Ireland at the Olympic Games, Helsinki, in the High Jump.

I send to you my congratulations and best wishes for your personal success and for that of the whole team.

President

1952 Helsinki Olympic Games, selection letter.

THE
THE
BRITISH OLYMPIC ASSOCIATION

The XVth Olympiad
HELSINKI, 1952

List of Great Britain's Competitors
Instructions to Team
Dates of Competitions
and
Table of Metric Equivalents

1952 Helsinki Olympic Games Team Handbook cover

Athletics (Men)—*Continued*

COMPETITORS

P. C. ALLDAY	K. E. JOHNSON
L. ALLEN	L. C. LEWIS
T. D. ANDERSON	A. W. LILLINGTON
E. McDONALD BAILEY	R. D. W. MILLER
R. G. BANNISTER	G. W. NANKEVILLE
C. W. BRASHER	F. NORRIS
C. J. CHATAWAY	A. B. PARKER
D. McD. CLARK	F. J. PARKER
G. W. COLEMAN	A. S. PATERSON
S. E. W. COX	R. C. PAVITT
M. J. DENLEY	J. H. PETERS
A. DICK	M. PHARAOH
J. I. DISLEY	D. A. G. PIRIE
E. C. K. DOUGLAS	F. SANDO
G. M. ELLIOTT	J. A. SAVIDGE
F. EVANS	A. W. SCOTT
L. EYRE	B. SHENTON
J. A. GILES	N. D. STACEY
D. K. GRACIE	D. A. TUNBRIDGE
J. A. GREGORY	A. WEBSTER
R. HARDY	P. WELLS
T. L. HIGGINS	C. T. WHITE
P. B. HILDRETH	G. B. R. WHITLOCK
G. L. IDEN	H. H. WHITLOCK
W. JACK	H. WHITTLE

ATHLETICS (Women)

OFFICIALS

Mrs. W. E. HUGHES ... ... }
Mrs. M. AMIES ... ... } *Assistant Team Managers*

COMPETITORS

Miss H. ARMITAGE	Miss T. E. HOPKINS
Miss S. CAWLEY	Miss A. E. JOHNSON
Miss S. CHEESEMAN	Mrs. S. LERWILL
Miss D. COATES	Miss P. G. SEABORNE
Miss J. C. DESFORGES	Miss O. SHIVAS
Miss P. Y. DEVINE	Miss P. A. THREAPLETON
Miss S. FARMER	Mrs. D. B. J. TYLER
Miss J. FOULDS	Mrs. C. L. WILLOUGHBY

219

1952 Helsinki Olympic Games Identity Card outside

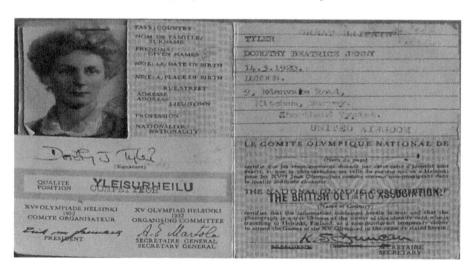

1952 Helsinki Olympic Games Identity Card inside

KORKEUSHYPPY
NAISET
Loppukilpailu

SAUT EN HAUTEUR, DAMES	HIGH JUMP, LADIES	HÖJDHOPP, DAMER
Finale	Final	Final

Riman korkeudet (sm): 135, 140, 145, 150, 155, 158, 161, 163, 165.

Heights of the bar (cm): 135, 140, 145, 150, 155, 158, 161, 163, 165.

Hauteurs de la barre: 1 m 35, 1 m. 40, 1 m. 45, 1 m. 50, 1 m. 55, 1 m. 58, 1 m. 61, 1 m. 63, 1 m. 65.

Ribbans höjd (cm): 135, 140, 145, 150, 155, 158, 161, 163, 165.

OSANOTTAJAT: PARTICIPANTES: COMPETITORS: DELTAGARE:

Nimi Nom Name Namn								
227 Tyler, Dorothy B. J.	G-B							
225 Hopkins, Thelma E.	G-B							
237 Mettal, Tamar	ISR							
831 Pöntinen, Seija T.	SF							
226 Lerwill, Sheila	G-B							
718 Ericsson, Solveig A.	SVE							
910 Modrachová, Olga	T-S							
367 Whitty, Alice A. D.	CAN							
366 Josephs, Dawn E.	CAN							
834 Heikkilä, Sisko S.	SF							
116 Brand, Esther C.	S-AF							
717 Larking, Gunhild M.	SVE							
287 Schenk, Feodora	AUT							
299 Russell, Kathleen M.	JAM							
489 Chudina, Aleksandra	USSR							
288 Sablatnig, Berta	AUT							
482 Košova, Nina	USSR							
483 Ganeker, Galina	USSR							
66 Jurdelina de Castro, Deise	BRA							

OLYMPIAVOITTAJA 1952:
Champion olympique 1952: Olympic Champion 1952: Olympisk segrare 1952:

2 ....

3 ....

4 ....

5 ....

6 ....

) 6 (

1952 Helsinki Olympic Games programme Event page,
Competition day

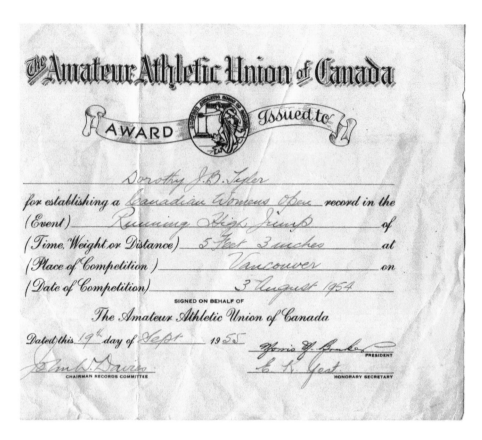

Canadian Open (All-Comers) record certificate

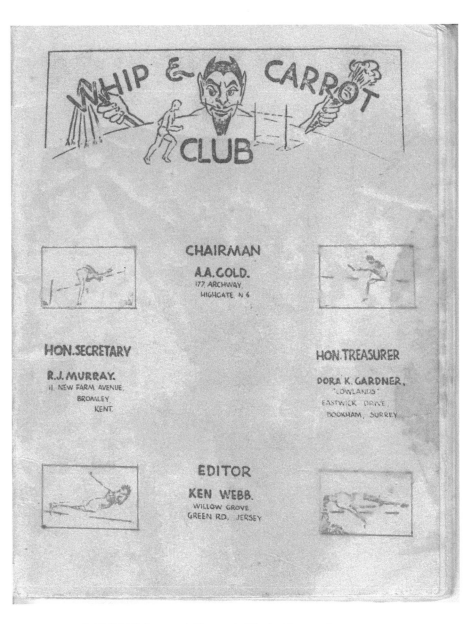

1955 Whip and Carrot Club Magazine cover

BRITISH AMATEUR ATHLETIC BOARD

(Affiliated to the I.A.A.F. as the governing Athletic Association for the United Kingdom of Great Britain and Northern Ireland)

Constituent Members:
AMATEUR ATHLETIC ASSOCIATION
SCOTTISH AMATEUR ATHLETIC ASSOCIATION
NORTHERN IRELAND AMATEUR ATHLETIC ASSOCIATION

President: H.R.H. THE DUKE OF EDINBURGH, K.G., K.T., G.B.E.

Hon. Secretary: J. C. G. CRUMP	*Clerk to the Board:* G. W. SMITH	*Hon. Treasurer:* H. M. ABRAHAMS

Telephone: LANgham 3498.
Telegrams: ATHLETE, WESTCENT, LONDON

54 TORRINGTON PLACE,
LONDON W.C.1

14th August, 1956.

It gives me much pleasure to invite, on behalf of the British Amateur Athletic Board Dorothy Tyler to represent Gt. Britain and Northern Ireland's Track and Field Team in the High Jump at the XVIth Olympic Games at Melbourne, 1956.

I congratulate you upon your selection and I send you my best wishes for success in your Olympic competition.

(signature)

1956 Melbourne Olympic Games selection letter

THE
BRITISH OLYMPIC ASSOCIATION

The XVIth Olympiad
MELBOURNE, 1956

List of Great Britain's Competitors
Instructions to Team
Dates of Competitions
and
Table of Metric Equivalents

1956 Melbourne Olympic Games Team handbook

225

Athletics (Men)—*Continued*

SANDO, Frank Dennis. (14.3.31.) 12 New Road, Ditton, Kent.
SANDSTROM, Eric Roy. (11.9.31.) 10 Helmsley Grove, Hull.
SHAW, Robert (Bob) Douglas. (27.12.32.) 21 Boxwell Road, Berkhamsted, Herts.
SHENTON, Brian. (15.3.27.) 77 Lovibonds Avenue, Orpington, Kent.
SHIRLEY, Eric. (3.4.29.) 41 Narcissus Road, London, N.W.6.
THOMPSON, Donald James. (20.1.33.) 1 Clevedon Gardens, Cranford, Hounslow, Middlesex.
VICKERS, Stanley Frank. (18.6.32.) 101 Shroffold Road, Downham, Bromley, Kent.
WELLS, Peter. (23.5.29.) 95, Main North Road, Amberley, North Canterbury, New Zealand.
WHEELER, Michael Keith Valentine. (14.2.35.) 7 Castle Street, Christchurch, Hants.
WILMSHURST, Kenneth Stanley David. (9.4.31.) 90 Claygate Lane, Hinchley Wood, Surrey.
WOOD, Kenneth. (21.11.30.) 186 Bramall Lane, Sheffield 2.

ATHLETICS—Women

OFFICIAL

Mrs. M. E. Amies ... ... *Assistant Team Manager*

COMPETITORS

ALLDAY, Suzanne. (26.11.34.) "Greenview," Leicester Village, Hove, Sussex.
ARMITAGE, Heather Joy. (17.3.33.) "Hatfield House," Hykeham Road, Lincoln.
BENNETT, Audrey Ethel. (1.4.36.) 133 Old Church Road, Chingford, Essex.
HOPKINS, Thelma Elizabeth. (16.3.36.) "Filey," Upper Malone, Belfast, N. Ireland.
HOSKIN, Sheila Hilary. (14.10.36.) London.
PASHLEY, Anne. (5.6.35.) Marine View Hotel, Great Yarmouth, Norfolk.
PAUL, June. (13.6.34.) 79 Aubert Court, Avenell Road, London, N.5.
QUINTON, Carole Louise. (11.7.36.) 37 Anchorage Road, Sutton Coldfield, Warwickshire.
SCRIVENS, Jean Eileen. (15.10.35.) 6A Wingford Road, Brixton Hill, London, S.W.2.
TYLER, Dorothy Jenny Beatrice. (14.3.20.) "Evergreen," 86 Ballards Way, South Croydon, Surrey.
WAINWRIGHT, Pauline Anne. (16.10.33.) 3 Wayside Crescent, Five Lane Ends, Bradford, Yorks.

17

1956 Melbourne Olympic Games Team handbook Athletics team page

226

1956 Melbourne Olympic Games. Identity card cover

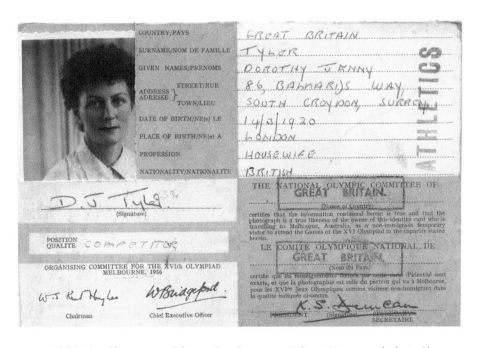

1956 Melbourne Olympic Games. Identity card detail.

HIGH JUMP (WOMEN)

QUALIFYING TRIALS
SAUT EN HAUTEUR (FEMMES)   SALTO DE ALTURA (MUJERES)

Previous Olympic Winners

		m.	ft.	in.
1928	E. Catherwood, Canada	1.59	5	2½
1932	J. Shiley, U.S.A.	1.65	5	5¼
1936	I. Csak, Hungary	1.60	5	3
1948	A. Coachman, U.S.A.	1.68	5	6¼
1952	E. Brand, South Africa	1.67	5	5¾

(Independent calculations)

World Record

1.75m.   5ft. 8¾in.   Y. Balas, Rumania, 14.7.1956, Bucharest, Rumania

Olympic Record

| 1948 | A. Coachman, U.S.A., | 1.68m. | 5ft. 6¼in. |
| 1948 | D. J. B. Tyler, Great Britain | 1.68m. | 5ft. 6¼in. |

The qualifying height is 1.58m. (5ft. 2¼in.). All competitors who attain this height will take part in the Final (Event 2—at 2.45 p.m.). If less than 12 competitors attain this height, then the 12 best competitors qualify.

Three consecutive failures, regardless of the height at which any of such failures occur, disqualify from further jumping; i.e., a competitor may forego his second and third jumps at a particular height (after failing first time) and still jump at a subsequent height.

568	McDaniel, M. L.	U.S.A.	545	Hopkins, T. E.	
561	Paternoster, P.	Italy			Great Britain & N. Ireland
557	Voborilova, J.	Czechoslovakia	556	Modrachova, O.	Czechoslovakia
559	Bennett, A. E.		554	Mason, M. M.	Australia
	Great Britain & N. Ireland		567	Flynn, A. M.	U.S.A.
564	Balas, Y.	Rumania	566	Larking, G. M.	Sweden
562	Donaghy, J. M.	New Zealand	552	Cooper, J.	Australia
555	Whitty, A. A.	Canada	558	Kilian, I.	Germany
553	Bernoth, C. E.	Australia	569	Pissareva, M.	U.S.S.R.
570	Ballod, V.	U.S.S.R.	560	Tyler, D. J. B.	
565	Geyser, H. L.	South Africa			Great Britain & N. Ireland
			690	Knapp, R.	Austria

3

The Most Hon. The Marquess of Exeter,
K.C.M.G.

President: ~~Lord Burghley, K.C.M.G.~~ (Great Britain)
Hon. Secretary-Treasurer: D.T.P.Pain.
(Great Britain)

P. Mericamp. (France)
L. Miettinen. (Finland)
A. Paulen. (Holland)
E. L. Albe. (Argentine)
N. Kalinin. (U.S.S.R.)
K. Křenický. (Czecho-Slovakia)
G. D. Sondhi. (India)
O. Tendeland. (Norway)
B. Zauli. (Italy)
D. J. Ferris. (U.S.A.)

Postal address:
    Halton House, 23, Holborn,
    London, E.C.1, England.
Telegraphic address:
    Marathon, London.
Telephone: Chancery 3419.

5th February   19 57.

Dear Mrs. Tyler,

I thank you for your letter of 18th January, in which you accuse me of deleting your name from the new World Record Book.

In point of fact, the deletion was made by the I.A.A.F. in their amendment to the official list of World Records issued in 1952 and the matter was evidently thoroughly investigated by my predecessor at that time.

However, since you feel that an injustice has been done to you, I will raise the matter at the next meeting of the Council and, no doubt, they will make a ruling.

Kind regards,

Yours sincerely,

Hon. Secretary-Treasurer.

Mrs. D. Tyler,
"Evergreen",
86 Ballards Way,
South Croydon, Surrey.

1957 IAAF Letter re dispute over Dorothy's world record.

1957 Arthur Gold's letter on track usage, craft and etiquette

Fanny Blankers-Koen
Amsteldijk 102'   Amsterdam, 13th June 1958

Dear Dorothy,

    It will be nice that Jan can go to your friends, who has a son
of his own age. You see he must learn to speak English well and the
best way is of course if he can stay with an English family. Jan
goes to England the 28th of July to the family Eric Kennell, 9 Pears
Close, Kenilworth, Warwickshire, phone Ken.1017. Till yet I don't
know the exact date how long he can stay with the Kennells, but I
suppose that as soon as he has arrived in Kenilworth he can phone you
or write you a letter. But before that thank your friends for their
offer and tell them, that we will be very glad if Sandy and Jill likes
to stay in Holland next year, that they are welcome.

    Otherwise I hope that you have received the names of the girls
who come to Mitcham. They are very enthousiastic and I hope that it
will be a nice meeting and that your team will come next year to Amsterdam. In the meanwhile,

                                    Sincerely yours,

1958 Fanny Blankers-Koen. Personal letter to Dorothy.

231

BRITISH AMATEUR ATHLETIC BOARD

Affiliated to the I.A.A.F. as the Governing Athletic Association for the United Kingdom of Great Britain and Northern Ireland)

Constituent Members:
AMATEUR ATHLETIC ASSOCIATION
SCOTTISH AMATEUR ATHLETIC ASSOCIATION
NORTHERN IRELAND AMATEUR ATHLETIC ASSOCIATION

President : H.R.H. THE PRINCE PHILIP, DUKE OF EDINBURGH, K.G., K.T., G.B.E.

Hon. Secretary	*Hon. Treasurer*	*Hon. Team Manager*	*Clerk to the Board*
J. C. G. CRUMP, O.B.E., J.P.	H. M. ABRAHAMS, C.B.E., J.P.	L. R. TRUELOVE	G. W. SMITH

Telephone : LANgham 3498
Telegrams : ATHLETE, WESTCENT, LONDON.

54, TORRINGTON PLACE,
LONDON,
W.C.1.

JCGC/MT.

17th April, 1959.

Mrs. D. J. Tyler,
'Eevergeen,'
86, Ballards Way,
South Croydon, Surrey.

PERSONAL AND CONFIDENTIAL.

Dear Dorothy,

As you know, His Royal Highness The Prince Philip, our President, is to preside over a meeting of the British Amateur Athletic Board to be held at the Hotel Rubens, Buckingham Palace Road, S.W. 1, on Wednesday May 20th. Prior to the commencement of the Board meeting, His Royal Highness will present World Record plaques to those athletes who have earned them during 1958.

Following the meeting, there will be a small tea party during which individuals who have rendered service to the Board, such as our Honorary Medical Officers, Honorary Transport Officer, Honorary Physiotherapist will attend in order that they may have the opportunity of meeting His Royal Highness.

We also feel that the representatives of the athletes on the Athletes Advisory Committee would welcome the opportunity of being present at this time and I am quite certain that His Royal Highness would welcome the opportunity of meeting them.

In these circumstances, I invite you to be at the Hotel Rubens at 4 p.m. on Wednesday May 20th. It is expected that the small tea party will commence about 4.15 p.m. and during this I shall have the opportunity, I hope, with His Royal Highness' permission, of presenting you to him.

I hope you will welcome this opportunity of being present and I would ask you to regard this matter as confidential for the time being, until I have received formal approval from Buckingham Palace that we may issue the

-over-

1959 BAAB invitation to presentation of world record plaques.

232

AMATEUR ATHLETIC ASSOCIATION
PATRON: HER MAJESTY THE QUEEN

President: The Most Hon. The Marquess of Exeter, K.C.M.G. LL.D.

Honorary Secretary   Honorary Treasurer
E.H.L. Clynes, O.B.E.   A.D. Thwaites
                          Assistant Secretary
                             G.W. Smith

                    A.A.A. COACHING COMMITTEE
                    Chairman: M.C. NOKES, M.C.

Honorary Secretary: Hon. Assistant Secretary
R. St. G.T. Harper   K.S. Duncan, M.B.E.

                                                54, Torrington Place,
                                                   LONDON, W.C. 1.

mrs. D.J. Syke   (Date as Postmark)
86, Ballards Way
East Croydon

Dear ~~Sir~~, Madam,

        This is to inform you that you have passed the Examination as
A.A.A. Honorary Coach in the following events:

        --------------------- Jumps --------------------------

        You have failed in: -----------------------------------

        I should like to take this opportunity of congratulating you
and wishing you every success in your Coaching activities.

        Should you wish to wear the A.A.A. Honorary Coach Vest Badge
and Lapel Badge, these can be obtained from the A.A.A. Offices at
the following prices:

                    Vest Badge .... 5s. each
                    Lapel   " .... 3s. "
                    Sew-on-   .... 1s. 9d. each

        Honorary Coaches' Gold Wire Blazer Badges are also now available,
price £1.11s. 6d. each.

        I am enclosing a brochure giving particulars of Instructional
Booklets which can be obtained from the A.A.A. Offices.

        I take it you will get in touch with the Honorary Coaching
Secretary for your County in due course.

                          Yours sincerely,

                          K.S. DUNCAN

                          Honorary Assistant Secretary
                             Coaching Committee.

1960 AAA letter re Honorary Coaching award

Dear Dorothy,

How nice to hear from you. I certainly should bring the matter
of the check mark up at your Southern Committee meeting and suggest
that they raise it with the A.A.A., who appointed the officials. I
am sure you will understand me if I say that I would like to hear
the views of the Referee and Judge before criticising what he did,
though I will say, at once, that I myself would have no hesitation
in permitting a mark on the run up, but not in meetings under
I.A.A.F. rules, in the pit itself. The A.A.A. still permit a mark
in the pit provided it is removed after the jump, but the I.A.A.F.
now specifically exclude this.

I think it could be argued that by implication the I.A.A.F. rules
do not permit a <u>competitor</u> to place check marks, since it says:
"No marks shall be placed in any jumping pit, but the <u>Organising
Committee</u> may place marks outside". On the other hand the beginning
of the rule (Rule 34 (7), permits a competitor to "place any marks
to assist him in his run up or take-off" and while again it can be
argued that this only applies to high-jumping, since the same rule
concludes " and a handkerchief on the cross-bar for sighting
purposes", in fact rule 7 is under the heading "General Rules" and
in no way limited to high jumping. I have not seen a competitor
place a handerchief on the pole vault cross-bar, but I think he
would be allowed to do so!!!

In any case rules are meant to assure fair competition and in
my view there is nothing unfair in using check marks.

I expect when the matter is raised with the A.A.A. it may find
its way to the Rules and Records Committee of which I am Chairman, and
I shall certainly want some convincing that the action could be
classified as an "unfair aid",

Yours ever,

Harold M. Abrahams

Not as so many officials
appear to think, to
penalise athletes

1961 Harold Abrahams' letter re high jump rules.

AMATEUR ATHLETIC ASSOCIATION

Founded 1880   Incorporated 1948

Patron : HER MAJESTY THE QUEEN

President : THE MOST HON. THE MARQUESS OF EXETER, K.C.M.G., LL.D.

Honorary Secretary
E. H. L. CLYNES, O.B.E.

Administrative Officer
L. A. G. HIGDON

Honorary Treasurer
P. S. GALE

Telephone : LANgham 3498
Telegrams : ATHLETE LONDON W 1

26, PARK CRESCENT,

LONDON,

W.1

Dear Mrs. Tyler,

<u>A.A.A. Honorary Senior Award.</u>   12th November, 1964.

<u>(International Athletes)</u>

On behalf of the Officers of The Association, I am very happy to inform you that you were successful at the Hon. Senior (Practical) Examination held at Carshalton, Surrey, on 8th November,1964 , being exempt from taking the Written Exam, and you are now a fully qualified A.A.A. Hon. Senior Coach.

We have recorded the following particulars and I should be glad if you would please verify, especially the section concerning address, and a stamped addressed questionnaire is attached for this purpose, which kindly complete and return as soon as possible.

<u>Name:</u>   D.J.B. TYLER   (MRS)   <u>Date Qualified:</u>   8.11.64.

<u>Address:</u>   86, Ballards Way, South Croydon, <u>Your Coaching Ref.No.</u> 619

<u>County/~~District No.~~</u> SURREY   <u>Event/s Passed:</u>   HIGH JUMP

I hope that you will find opportunities to coach some athletes, particularly those of a high standard, and to assist on Coaching Courses.

I feel sure that your County/~~District~~ Hon. Coaching Secretary, P.C.Tomkins, 15, Ashridge Way, Morden, Surrey.

and your Area Hon. Coaching Secretary:

D.J. Hayward, 36, Primrose Road, South Woodford, E.18.

will be very interested to know of your success, and will be glad to assist you to make the best use of your outstanding abilities.

To ensure prompt receipt of the 'Coaching Newsletter' and to keep our records up-to-date, would you please notify me of any change of address in future.

Mr. John Salisbury, The Hon. Secretary of the I.A.C., has been notified of your success and I'm sure he will be very pleased.

Yours sincerely,

S. Strickland

Coaching Administrator.

1964 AAA letter re Honorary Senior Coaching award

AMATEUR ATHLETIC ASSOCIATION

HONORARY SENIOR COACHING AWARD

Authorisation to purchase Honorary Senior Coach Badges from
Mr. J. Hitchcock, (A.A.A. Publications Sales Centre),
39, Saxonbury Avenue, Sunbury-on-Thames, Middlesex.

NAME: MRS. D.J.B. TYLER

COACHING REFERENCE NO. 619 (SENIOR COACH)

Authorised by E. STRICKLAND, O.B.E., COACHING ADMINISTRATOR

Please enclose this Card when ordering Badges from our
Sales Centre, which will be returned with your order.

1964 AAA authorisation to purchase coaching badge card

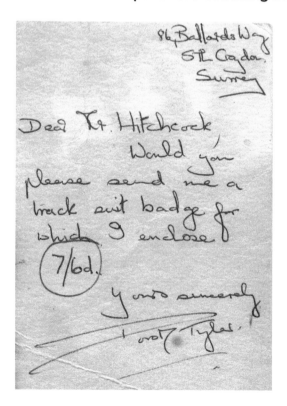

86 Ballards Way
S. Croydon,
Surrey

Dear Mr. Hitchcock,
Would you
please send me a
track suit badge for
which I enclose
7/6d.

Yours sincerely

Dorothy Tyler.

1964 Dorothy's coaching badge request

Team Manager

Wettkampfprotokoll

Leichtathletik-Länderkampf

DDR - England

Damen und Herren

am 4. und 5. September 1965 in Berlin

Friedrich-Ludwig-Jahn Stadion

1965 DDR v England match protocol document cover

1967 Book cover. Teaching of athletics in school and club by Dorothy

Coach and athlete, Dorothy and Eleanor Rowe Athletics
Weekly cover 1969

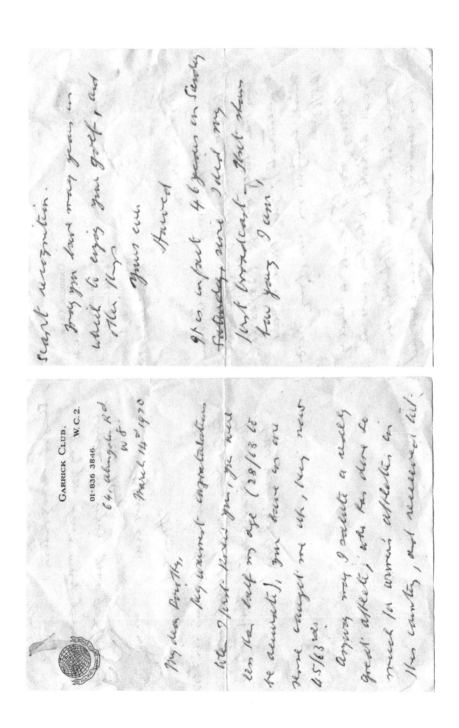

1970 Harold Abrahams' congratulation letter for Dorothy's 50th birthday.

Mrs D.J.Tyler MBE
51 Ridge Langley
Sanderstead
Surrey CR2 0AP
Tel: 020 8651 3070

13/7/11

Dear John,

Thank you for your letter and news. I met Terry Godwin on a cruise last year and he is in touch with Brian Hewson.

They have told me that I will get two tickets free and can buy two, but I will be sent an application form, that was weeks ago.,

I've had to give golf trapped a nerve while playing and that turned int sciatica.

Remember me anyone whose still around. Yours sincerely D & D

Letter from Dorothy to John Brett

241

January 30th 2012

The London Marathon Limited
PO Box 1234
London SE1 0XT
Telephone: 020 7902 0200
Facsimile: 020 7620 4208
Website: www.virginlondonmarathon.com

Dorothy Tyler MBE
51 Ridge Langley
Sanderstead
Surrey
CR2 0AP

Dear Dorothy

It was great to talk to you on Friday regarding you agreeing to be the starter of the London Marathon on April 22nd. I also understand that you will be accompanied by Dick.

We will arrange to pick you up at 07.30 and bring you and Dick directly to the Marathon start at Blackheath where you will arrive at 08.15 and be met by myself and John Spurling our Chairman.

There are 3 races to start: Elite Women 09.00, Wheelchair 09.20 and Elite Men and masses 09.45. You will then be driven to the Finish in time to see the races finish. We will then drive you both home at about 12.45.

You mentioned that you could wear your 1948 OG outfit and I think this is a great idea. If you have any further questions please call me on 07721 428083. I will speak to you nearer the race to make sure that you are happy with the arrangements.

I hope that you enjoy your day with us.

Yours sincerely

Barry

Dave Bedford
Joint Race Director

cc. Nick Bitel

Invitation to be the Starter of the 2012 London Marathon

Appendix H
BARRY'S TRIBUTE TO HIS MOTHER

The text of the address that Barry Tyler gave at his mother's funeral at the West Suffolk Crematorium on 17 October 2014.

"Welcome everyone.

From her mother, a professional dancer and her father, a cricketing fast bowler, Dorothy inherited strength, speed, flexibility and a great deal of spring! She showed amazing self-determination from an early age. She joined Mitcham Athletic Club following success in school competitions and progressed in a short time to winning the Olympic High Jump silver medal in Berlin at the tender age of 16 years. She had no manager, no agent, no parental support and no coach until 1950, yet she won two Olympic silver medals, two Empire (Commonwealth) gold medals and broke the high jump world record during this time.

In breaking the record, she managed to jump above her own height, which in those days was a very brave thing to do as there was only 2" of sand to land in; hitting or knocking off the triangular metal bar could cause injury and long spikes on trainers were always a danger during take off or landing.

Mum described herself as a bit of a rebel and when she was told by the women' AAA not to wear such short shorts, she retorted, 'if they were longer, they would knock the bar off!' She also used her status to defend the rights of women athletes when she wrote to the 1948 Olympic committee complaining that they should increase the number of events in which women could compete and not as had been proposed, reduce them. They did as she said!

After the war, she pioneered changing people's perception of what women athletes could achieve. She showed the medical experts that after having children, women could continue to do strenuous exercise and compete for many years and that in fact they could become stronger.

When David and I were very young, Mum's athletic career kept her away from home a great deal. She seemed to us like a film star with her long blond hair, but we enjoyed having a famous mother and there were many benefits.

Press interest meant that we had a wonderful pictorial record of our childhood with many pictures showing us playing in large sandpits (between jumps of course!).

We attended athletic venues both home and abroad and they were like big adventure playgrounds.

She brought back many interesting and unusual presents from abroad and we were always very attentive when she opened her suitcase.

Our best adventure was to travel with mum and dad across Europe to the Rome Olympics where we were able to attend the athletics almost every day!

Although she encouraged us a great deal, unfortunately David and I did not inherit her international ability but we have enjoyed a lifelong love of sport and participation.

Mother often spoke in a forthright way but could be very amusing with a mischievous smile on her face.

Following her retirement from athletics, my mother joined my father, playing golf and they were members of Croham Hurst golf club for many years enjoying some success. She was able to give him lots of encouraging advice!

She was awarded the MBE in 2002 given to her by Prince

Charles. He said to her 'You have been a long time coming' to which she replied 'You have been a long time asking'.

Also when receiving the Sportswriter's Lifetime Achievement Award, she stole the show by accusing Dick Fosbury of being a cheat because he jumped over the bar head first and when everyone copied him, they broke all her records!

For 20 years she worked as a volunteer in the Mind charity shop and it was somewhat fitting that she was invited to model in her Olympic vest, holding the 1936 Olympic torch that had been left outside a London charity shop, to advertise its auction. Having held the torch she decided she would like it and a successful bid was achieved.

In 2012 she was the official starter of the London Marathon. She was overjoyed to see the mass of runners, particularly the women. It was confirmation to her that her efforts to change the restrictions in women's sport had been worthwhile. What a legacy!

Finally, mother loved family gatherings and visits to and from family. She loved being involved with her grandchildren and seeing her great grandchildren gave her great pleasure.

She had a long, interesting and wonderful life and saw a lot of the world. She had an amazing husband, my father, who loved and supported her throughout her life and career. She was an inspiration to all".

Acknowledgements

The Tyler Family, Dorothy, Dick, Barry and David

Athletics Australia — Personal Contacts

Shirley Berry née Cawley, Olympian — Great Britain Olympians

John Brant, National Union of Track Statisticians — Women's performance statistics

John Brett, Mitcham AC — Memories and Historical material

Chris Brightman, Croham Hurst Golf Club — Memories

Matthew Brown, London Marathon — Photo, Dorothy starting London Marathon

Lorna Boothe, Olympian, Coach and Team Manager — Memories

Christine Bower, British Olympic Association — Statistics

Ottavio Castellini, IAAF — World record Statistics

Alice Chandler — Acrylic illustrations

Laura Coster, Old Palace School of John Whitgift — Students' artwork

Lynn Cowlard, Mitcham AC — Memories

Pam Davies, Croham Hurst Golf Club — Memories

Sylvia Disley, née Cheeseman, Olympian — Memories

Fritz Emmert — German archive material and translation

Nicola Fleet — Indexing and photographic scanning

Dick Fosbury, Olympian — Foreword

Alec Fruin, Mitcham AC — Photo Badge and archive material

Brian Hewson, Mitcham AC Olympian — Memories

Thelma Hopkins, Olympian — Memories

Mike Hughes	Photographic enhancement
Irish Hockey Federation	Contact liaison
Job King, England Athletics	Photo Dorothy and Dick Fosbury
Ian Lamont, Croydon Advertiser	Initial introduction
Sheila Lerwill, Olympian	Memories and photo identification
Steve Mackinson, Croham Hurst Golf Club	Golfing contacts
Peter Matthews, National Union of Track Statisticians	Dorothy Tyler Statistics
Stephanie Moreno, IOC Olympic Studies Centre	1952 Helsinki Olympic Information
Olympic Museum Berlin	1936 Archive photos and material
Olympic Museum Lausanne	1936 and 1952 Archive photos and material
Antony Owers, Hon. British Consul, Curacao	1949 Port of call research
Dorothy Parlett née Manley, Olympian	Memories and photographs
Bill Payne, Mitcham AC / Sutton and District AC	Memories
Vivienne Rawlinson, Croham Hurst Golf Club	Memories
Aileen Regan	Proof Reading
Bernie Regan	Editing
Chris Scott	Flight information
Wilfried Spronk, DLV	German archive material
Trevor Vincent, Athletics Australia	Photographs
UK Athletics	Contacts
Gwenda Ward née Matthews, Olympian	Memories
Mel Watman, National Union of Track Statisticians	Proof reading
Alice Whitty, Olympian	Memories

Thelma Wright, Athletics Canada   Personal contacts

Acknowledgement has been credited wherever possible,
and any omissions are due to absence of provenance.

Book References

Athletics Weekly

Athletics World, Volume 1   Norris and Ross McWhirter

Berlin Games. How Hitler won the war   Guy Walters

Berlin Olympic Games 1936   The Official BOA Report

Berlin Olympic Games 1936   Organising Committee Report

British Women's Athletics, Part 2 - Peter R Pozzoli
International 1921-64)

Helsinki Olympic Games 1952   The Official BOA Report

High Jump NUTS Survey   Ian Tempest

History of Mitcham AC   Alec Fruin

London Olympic Games 1948   The Official Report of the Organising
Committee

Lady Icarus   Lindie Naughton

Meet the Olympians   Dimiter Mishev

Melbourne Olympic Games 1956   The Official BOA Report

Olympic Odyssey 1956   edited Stan Tomlin

Progression of IAAF Records   IAAF

Queen of the Track   Heather Lang

Running Round The World, Courtesy Robert Jack Crump
Hale and Co

Sportsman's Who's Who   Raymond Glendenning and Robert
Bateman

Track and Field Omnibus   J Kenneth Doherty

Whip and Carrot Club Magazine   Ken Webb (Editor)

With the Skin of their Teeth   G. O. Nickalls

Women's Athletics   George Pallett

Other Article

Scandal about "Dora" and the "Bergmann   Journal of Olympic History, Dec 2009
Case"

Index

Lightning Source UK Ltd.
Milton Keynes UK
UKOW07f0809090915

258340UK00014B/51/P